Usha Akella writes with "Sanskrit mantras in her veins," from an exceedingly broad perspective—as feminist, activist, organizer, poet-citizen, engaging an intellect profoundly contemporary with the times. She spans a long reach, from the looming questions and fears around our intense and out of control pandemic to India's national trauma in the Delhi rape case.

"Each of us is a naïve question as we always have been / curved like an embryo." She also writes wittily her version of WC Williams's 'This is Just to Say', where "plums are prudish / slow to ripen / a bit stiff." She probes, she thinks with each situation, she grapples with the world in all its manifestations, also as a mother, poised in anticipation of what may come, but always with a steady heart and hand and ear in poetry. One line sent chills up my spine, as she contemplates all kinds of extinctions. An image of Virginia Woolf "inching into the Ouse."

We are truly at precipice and this poetry can help wake up the world to itself. Kudos.

— Anne Waldman, author of *Trickster Feminism*

In *I Will Not Bear You Sons*, poetry, the ordinary, and the extraordinary are all part of the same whole—spirituality. Usha Akella is an activist and a sage, confronting us with images of oppression while the spirit of Sanskrit mantras runs in her veins. "I wanted lakes to drink from, and they took the moisture from my body." Here we have a narrator who pays attention to her emotions and ideas and speaks freely. Each part of this collection is an interrogation, forcing us to embrace what the poem is transforming.

Deploying the full range of poetic license, the poet makes Kali, the Virgin Mary, and Kim Kardashian dance the ordinary into divinity. Most importantly, the poetic voice is secure in knowing she will not bear patriarchy any sons; instead, she will have patriarchy bear her words!

The sage in her sees difficulties as points of entry into devotion; the prayers are her poems. She does not wait for the clouds to deliver the divine; she rushes into the crowds to find it. These poems distil perennial wisdom and are charged with life and a brilliance that lends us humans, particularly women, a voice. The poet demands that we speak.

—Marianela Medrano, author of *Rooting: A Selection of Bilingual Poems*

Usha Akella has authored nine books that include poetry, a chapbook, and musical dramas. She earned a Master of Studies in Creative Writing from the University of Cambridge, UK. She was selected as a Creative Ambassador for the City of Austin for 2019 and 2015. Her work has been included in the *Harper Collins Book of English Poetry* (ed. Sudeep Sen, 2012). She read with a group of eminent South Asian Diaspora poets at the House of Lords in June 2016. She is an award-winning poet published widely and has featured at numerous prestigious international poetry festivals.

She is the founder of *Matwaala* (www.matwaala.com) and hosts the interview and conversations website (www.the-pov.com). *Matwaala* is the first South Asian Diaspora Poets Festival dedicated to increasing the visibility of diaspora poets in the USA that she co-directs with Pramila Venkateswaran. She is also the founder of the Poetry Caravan in New York and Austin which takes poetry readings to disadvantaged audiences in women's shelters, senior homes, hospitals.

Other books

**Poetry**
*Crossed Out in Red (Rubaiyat)* (2021)
*The Waiting* (2019)
*Ordinary* (2017)
*The Rosary of Latitudes* (2015)
*Come Back to Me Old and Gray* (2013)
*A Face that Does not Bear the Footprints of the World* (2008)
*… Kali Dances, So Do I …* (2000)

**Musical Drama**
*The Way of the Storm, an English Musical Drama on the Life of Meera Bai* (2020)
*Ek, An English Musical on the Life of Shri Shirdi Sai Baba* (2012)

**Edited Books and Journals**
*City of My Heart, Poetry on Hyderabad by Hyderabad Poets* (2021)
*Lucy's Platform* (Online Journal, 2019–present)
*Borderlands, Texas Poetry Review: Special Feature on Contemporary Macedonian Poets* (2007)
*en(compass). The Poetry Caravan Anthology* (2005)

# I WILL NOT BEAR YOU SONS

## Usha Akella

SPINIFEX

First published by Spinifex Press, 2021

Spinifex Press Pty Ltd
PO Box 5270, North Geelong, VIC 3215, Australia
PO Box 105, Mission Beach, QLD 4852, Australia

women@spinifexpress.com.au
www.spinifexpress.com.au

Edited by Susan Hawthorne and Pauline Hopkins
Cover design by Deb Snibson, MAPG
Typesetting by Helen Christie, Blue Wren Books
Typeset in Albertina
Printed by McPherson's Printing Group

A catalogue record for this
book is available from the
National Library of Australia

ISBN: 9781925950281 (paperback)
ISBN: 9781925950298 (ebook)

PEFC Certified
This product is from
sustainably managed forest
and controlled sources.
Recognised in Australia by
Responsible Wood.
PEFC/21-31-16     www.pefc.org.au

# Gratitude

Remembering,

Jem Poster at the University of Cambridge whose able guidance helped to first forge the poems into the glimmer of a book.

Pramila Venkateswaran and Sophia Naz for reading the manuscript and offering astute feedback.

Anne Waldman and Marianela Medrano for endorsing the book. Their own words are torches lighting the path.

Translators, festival and reading series' directors, journal editors and publishers, who showcased poems.

Ravi, Anannya, Phanni—husband, daughter and brother—my family, my pillars who allow me to rage, age, create, write and be. Their unfaltering support and care carry me through.

Specially,

Spinifex Publishers, Susan Hawthorne and Renate Klein and Senior Editor Pauline Hopkins for believing in my work and nurturing it to manifestation. To Maralann Damiano, Rachael McDiarmid, and Caitlin Roper. And to internal designer and typesetter, Helen Christie, thanks.

Cover designer, Deb Snibson, for her stunning cover artwork; her openness to incorporating the Sri Chakra, symbol of the goddess, so finely—deeply meaningful to me and cherished.

Always,

all my women friends, poets and spiritual guides for sustaining me with guidance, strength, sisterhood and friendship. I am ever indebted.

Dedicated to:

The Feminine
*all her names, forms, aspects and expressions*

# Contents

# Author's note

This book was not easy to write; it was a book I owed to the sex I am. I understand the feminine is the node for life on our planet—how feminism is related to religion, law, politics, culture, consumerism, society, caste, community, economics and the environment. For my poems to speak authentically, I have to speak *my* truth, however hard it is. I am bewildered by the fear and hate of women that is so cellularly entrenched in men it instigates bestiality, numbness, indifference and cruelty. That patriarchy is so cancerous it spurs women to inflict cruelty on their own sex unconscious to their roles as perpetrators. East or West, North or South, the perversion of the feminine is a staple on our planet—her exploitation occurs in every realm from political to spiritual.

These poems began to take shape formally as my second-year writing thesis at the University of Cambridge in 2017–18—thereon, expanding in scope, it evolved into the present collection. They are thematically united by feminism, activism and autobiography. By *autobiography*, I indicate the relationship of memoir to poetry—and abandon the uneasy literary term *confessional*, pregnant with Catholic Christian theology concepts of sin and guilt. I pay tribute to women, in the second section by addressing various issues like foot binding, FGM, rape, mysticism, politics, terrorism—hoping to rewrite a narrative of patriarchy and selfhood defined by the Brahmin Niyogi sensibility I was born into, and inculcated with.

I do not know when the spirit of these poems found me. Was it the very second I entered this world as a female infant close to midnight as the rain pelted the tiled rooftops in Eluru? Was it when my family returned to India from Australia and I became aware of a confusing culture that had contradictory prescriptions? Was it my adolescent years in Hyderabad when I began to realize that India's social norms for women were vastly different from her transcendental Vedantic truths? As I grew into womanhood, to a 'marriageable age', I became aware of a suffocating machinery in place that defined who or what a good girl was and how she ought to look, behave and be. This machinery seemed to pervert, impact or morph women's sensibilities and behavior. My body and soul became a battleground between India's spirituality, her social prescriptions and my innate sense of self. I became a chronic asthmatic; my body and mind has broken down many times in the past few decades under the weight of issues it processes. The horrors and hypocrisies of patriarchy are deep—I have personally encountered it in its family, dating and arranged marriage systems. Women's betrayals of each other has not been addressed enough in patriarchal systems. A sex that is divided will never be able to free itself unless it speaks with one voice. In these poems I discover a language for pain that has been a staple of my life.

When I moved to the USA I found another version of patriarchy—one that calls women to be a size zero, forcing an extreme body consciousness regulated by media prescriptions of beauty and an oversized cosmetic industry; a gender-view that manifests issues of violence against women, women and girl trafficking, a drug, alcohol and sex culture, objectification of women, pornography, date rape etc. A West that had seemed so glossy and liberated from far away was as deceptive as a 4-color ad. In some ways, the Hindu sensibility formed by a spirituality, myth and religion suffused with multiple goddesses is more deeply aware of the sacred feminine principle in life—even though, paradoxically, it has not curbed the entrenched patriarchy irrespective of caste and community.

Every battle waged for personal dignity is for me and my daughter— to give her a world more equal than the one I was shaped in. I owe her the fight so she can breathe easier, less encumbered by structures scripted by men for men. Every day is an opportunity for self-awareness, self-correction and self-emergence. I thank my husband Ravi for trying hard to raise a daughter without the crippling parts of our culture that stunt the female spirit. I know we tried hard.

I derive my courage from the courage of women writers like Sylvia Plath, Meena Kandasamy, Kamala Das, Ayaan Hirsi Ali, Pramila Venkateswaran and Neela Saxena. To the indomitable and tireless work done by so many for the betterment of girls and women, I humbly add these poems. Thank you, Spinifex for making the inchoate dream real.

—Usha Akella, 2021

I

## Ka     Ba     Akh

I wanted lakes to drink from and they took the moisture from my body,

"She breathes,"     they said,        and        prepared me for burial,

took my mind delicately through my nostrils,

I was light as a leaf       I made no sound.

"Leave the heart," he said,        she must feel this pain,

And all around me joy and laughter in jars watching like falcons and jackals.

They took my eyes          and gave me kohl,
took my hands    I grew claws
they gave me wings coated with wax,
took my womb        gave me myrrh,
and the linen they wound and wound,
and the days they wound and the hours of my life,
and my desires they wound and I lay there without a sound,
you need not be Egyptian they said *woman* is enough to be wound,
they carved out my vagina and stacked it as a pyramid pointing high.

And my daughter wailed *mummy mummy mummy*.

And the sand blew about and blew about       they call the sand civilization.

When I was white strips and dunked in resin and magical chants,

when I was anything but woman    they said,        "Go on,

even life here is not enough       you are not yet judged."

Plying me with virtue and riches to hand over to the Gods.

Caw Caw! I flew black beady-eyed bird,

the gods then raped me one by one with conundrums.

3

# From a Brahmin Niyogi Woman to a White Woman

I didn't dye my hair blue
I didn't say fuck you!

        I didn't become bisexual
bipolar alcoholic or metrosexual
I didn't try heroin

weed or morphine

   And yet, and yet
      I came apart   a part here and there
one sitting on the ground
         one on a chair

I don't have AIDS or irritating things
down there, I've stayed monogamous and true
I've been a good girl
I've kept my chastity like a pearl

And yet I rue, I am sad and rue
You see, I haven't done the things you do

I haven't woken up in strange beds
I've never been led

through back alleys
where the dirty things and other things carry on

You see, I am strong, and my head's not gone

Sanskrit mantras in my veins
Annamayya kirtanas are inner strains

I didn't fully come apart
somehow there is enough glue
       And yet I rue, I rue

I didn't fully come apart
        I'm waiting for my cue
To live my life like you

I haven't partied in the night
I haven't cursed the light

I haven't taken what's not mine
I know where to draw the line

The men I know know I'm mine

I haven't waited tables

        I'm always served

        Stable, always stable
I've never fully come apart

Only a part here and there
             And even though some
parts keenly smart
               I've never fully come apart

I watch your men trace your neckline
Look into your eyes and dance
I watch your romance
And wonder what it's like

        His eyes on your lips
Desire on your finger tips
   Your cleavages that you show
            Your ongoing tango

And wonder at you gays, and lesbians
And what is it you do
                          And how and who and what is true
                    And how you drop out of school

And you with husbands one two and three
          merry and so bloody free

And how you wed and divorce
     drifting from the source

               or so we think
          Who is it that really sinks?

I wonder about your lives          across the line

different different so damn different from mine

You live it out and about
With a scream and a shout

               While I, I'll tell you this
a secret in my fist
I live it all in my skin
 Incongruous as a purple elephant on a pencil tip

          I play charades within with all my parts
And one aches more than the rest
It's my aching heart

I see how you somehow do it as you like

And I am safe, safe I know
guided by theory of reap and sow
I keep myself pure as snow

I live in my suburban home
yellow stucco and stone
and the stones in my pockets grow

I stay within glass walls
where duty and goodness call

tipsy on dharma resisting booze

watching
      watching as they crack and break

watching Virgina Woolf inching to the Ouse.

# 7.8 Billion Caved

1.

This one looks like a planet of red windmills whirring
or a field of poppies, a wild corona of a star, heart of sunflower,
this pretty thing is fanged, arsenal in Death's stockpile,
small unseen things are perfectly precise,
Hanuman burnt the city of Lanka eroding pride.

2.

The bush is bursting with red berries,
spring has slipped through crevices breathing green on the city,
a musician plays his oud to the sky in himself,
the trees are gravestones to the forgotten dead,
the deer conglomerate driven to community,
families staked by windows notice the heartbeat of nature.

3.

The camera has vertigo, it's crazy arc
leering on the hoarded splendor of one family,
(what madness to record and pridefully share?)
lines of bottles on the kitchen cabinetry
riddled with oil of bright urine hue,
toilet rolls, bounties, tissues, food cans,
a pantry full of debris for doomsday,
this raid of the innards of stores,
this Freud's Id of fear and self, first.

4.

Where do we send our unclaimed sorrow?
The unlabeled debris of life?
The racking cough of unprocessed wounds?
There is no island to send them off, be done, be free.
Like those lines of caskets in dirt in Hart Island,
where New York City is belching unclaimed bodies,
its gut overflowing.

5.

The mind is like an abacus now
computing deaths on the excel sheet
of consciousness; from the Spanish flu 20–50 million,
from the Black Plague 50 million, from Covid …
what black hole continues to gorge up souls
or is it an empyrean of hopeful light,
what joust happens in the universe's annals
between what forces, this unending play
into and out of life, where is that mighty
being who once gave the song of life
to a tremulous warrior's heart in the middle of battle?
Each of us is a naive question as we have always been
curved like an embryo, full-stopped by death.

# Reemergence

We retreat and reemerge from our rooms
like waves meeting by the shore of the window,
this dance of three happens daily now—
needles crocheting a new pattern of reality.
Simple human actions, eating together, washing dishes,
of harmony, kinship and family—we are reconfigured
in a lucent house breathing a cornucopia of light,
limpid walls and tiles seem fluid like water
rippling a chiaroscuro, outside,
that—the red streak of a cardinal's winged surge,
that—the squirrels scampering on serrated trunks,
that—the unhurried drift of a dandelion
there, here, everywhere—the pandemic.

Spring is upon us—this too is reality—
the sun's golden bombarding drenching suffusing,
this beauty is undeniable—a world savaged by light
saved by light, singing with light,
rains baptize the streets asking us to rise anew,
the streets are rivers cupping reflections of the oaks and cedars,
blue bonnets and Indian paintbrush splatter the streets,
scarlet berries bud like miniature poppies on the dark green
and—a red whirring virus leaving shadows of painful stories,
this war unfolds as wars have always ravaged the earth,
some mine woe for profit,
some simply try to keep bone and skin together,
the human mind is rarely pellucid,
we understand what we can
and mostly move on in acceptance.

## Scuttlebutt

Sailors, across the Atlantic we stagger in vertigo trips,
careening, never cleaned of our baggage and past, the journey is
upbound, it seems most of the time with the
tattle of the waves murmuring our histories, what's the
tell tail in all of this? The direction of the wind?
Lateral systems in undulating latitudes do not aid.
Embayed, we belong to two lands and as the flag of the water erodes the
bulkhead of our hearts, we begin to belong nowhere.
Unshipped, we are exiled from anything that spells home.
Three sheets to the wind, each of us a paralyzed hulk in the hands of a
timoneer, perhaps, seasick himself of the voyages he charts.

Scuttlebutt: rumor/gossip/a nautical term for a casket of water or fountain around which
    sailors gather.
Careen: tilting a ship on its side to clean it.
Upbound: a vessel traveling upstream.
Tell Tail/Tell Tale: a light piece of string, yarn, rope or plastic.
Lateral systems: a system of aids to navigation.
Embayed: where a sailing ship is confined between two capes by a wind blowing
    on shore.
Bulkhead: an upright wall within the hull of a ship. Particularly a watertight,
    load-bearing wall.
Unship: to remove from a vessel.
Three sheets to the wind: the three sheets in the mast, if loose, will result in the ship
    meandering aimlessly downwind / A sailor who has drunk strong spirits beyond his capacity.
Timoneer: from the French timonnier, is a name given, on particular occasions,
    to the steersman of a ship.

## This Is Just to Say to William Carlos Williams

I have not eaten the plums
nor has my daughter.

The mangoes win, gluttonous yellow,
plump with scathing summers,
childhood's innocence,
moist memories
of dead grandmothers,
bellowing grandfathers,
the sweet homesickness,
a sticky dribble on the chin.

The plums are prudish,
slow to ripen, a bit stiff,
in the back of the fridge,
they are not delicious or sweet
though cold, I admit.

Your plums, Carlos,
Where do they come from?

# Poems I Can't Write

I am cracked glass glinting
in the crevices of the tar body of Kali,

I am gulped by fear
to say: this cleaved being is me,
but what option but to be severed,
a bold stump instead of
giddy caged flight,
                        in the mirror's polished night.

To be a kept woman in culture's gnarled comfort
or to be exiled, to breathe something that is something like air.

If you hold me—you cut yourself,
nothing nice, these poems,
not roses but spice, Eastern spices wafting across
a bipolar blue shaft you call the Atlantic, turning it yellow,
the color of turmeric staining transcendence and your
Mary's pristine robe glittering with stars above,
So glittering she didn't leave any light for us to shine,
how can we compete with that kind of glory?

So, I took another story called Kali,

garlanded with the skulls of
each painful fall in the world;
                        this is *our* bounty to share,
we stick out our tongue at countries that try to claim us,
inhabiting each like a ghoul inhabits a cremation ground for we
are never wholly human in each of them      this is our domain,
not among the stars. We hurt and are hurt, each step leaves a claw mark
on the sand, because pain is guttural, it belongs to the
subterranean      ask Mary when she lost her son, her cries flung, far flung
echoing in your own white souls 2000 years later, you paint your faces in vain.

And there is one version of her: beheading her own head
to survive—fountainous blood-gush,
Indian women do this, beheading and beheaded … read that
metaphor any way you want, it will break your heart,
that's the architecture of woman.

Her garment of hands reminding us
we make our own fates, or so we think
Does she not wear us all?
That grand goddess of eternity, she wears you too Mary,
Mary tell me, clad in your robe so blue so gossamer do you
ever meet her, do your paths cross, do you lift crosses together?

My poems bloom from cow dung soil,
'gobbar' we call it, spreading it thick on
walls of huts, the sun above so full of desire
alchemizing anything noble into something darker,

> Listen. I tell myself. Unburden
> yourself in these poems,
> say it to yourself: this cleaved self is I,
> victim, abuser, wreaking revenge
> senselessly on a battlefield, hurt,
> hurting, hating, fatigued. emerging.
> This is I. I am not vanquished.

I come from a hot land of famines and flood,
and ageless ancient sages meditating
in the cold summits of the Himalayas,
rarefied above, above a woman's body,
a country with veins of hidden tales that don't die,
nothing of the glory of outsourced capital profits
or soft wares you sell to us or we to you
white white people with wide blue eyes
not all poems are missives
but missing boats on the Ganges.

To speak these poems of heart-thaw
is time coming apart like organza sari pleats
stained with blood, turmeric and masalas,
generational-neurosis ripened to fully raging flowers
in my head, I am crowned with these poems, thorns
pressing into my forehead      oh no the tales are not dead,
my appetites are not fed,
and there is no second coming of light only the blight
of women staking the earth,
taking their own in every possible way,
and the innocent fall on some days,
and I am saying it with poems I can't write.

## I Will Not Bear You Sons

*What can a door deliver?*

The setting of this poem is innocuous—at the door,
A door is innocent of its exits and entrances,
What can a door deliver?
Hellos, bye-byes, blessings, Namaste, a peck on the cheek …

An open door can be the hole in a noose.

I had just celebrated his seventieth birthday,
decorating the house so, so, fit to welcome a God,
the saris draped on the ceiling, cascading rainbows
falling from the sky,
we wore our finery, our ornaments
as if the earth was liberated from every evil.

The food was laid out—kitchen-labor, labor of forgiveness,
I will not waste words on the menu
for I must speak of women, wombs and India.

A poem can glisten like a fresh wound.

In his speech he praised his wife,
his daughter, his sons, his grandchildren,
he omitted his daughters-in-law, and I
stilled my voice on the verge of bleeding red like a period,
and they ate and ate and danced and smiled and smirked,
and all was well with the world.

At the door we said our farewells,
like a *rangoli* I didn't know where I began and where I ended,
our smiles were the flames of Diwali lamps,
our foreheads marked with *sindoor*, this parting
gesture of farewell, blessing and fortune, our tie with
tradition, our comfort warm, our hearts glad, and then his
parting words as he paused at the threshold of departure—
"I want a grandson. This is my desire," he said to me.
"Give me a son," begs of my womb to do magic,
waiting for a juicy-fruit of a promise,
I was meant to swell and touch his feet in gratitude,
this is his blessing,
the nearest to affection in ten years.

A request can be a Sudarshan chakra shredding you.

The saris swayed in my mind
drained of color like shrouds,
shrieked the pallor of my silence—
the granddaughters, daughter, wife and the daughters-in-law
became carcasses salted with Hindu culture
spiced with clichés we've seen on Bollywood screens.

India! Your hand reached us again like Dusasanna,
disrobed us to stand in the glare
of our sex—woman, vagina, buttocks, breasts and braids,
never good enough until unclothed by men,
my daughter erased like a misspelling by his desire.

The walls were unblinking as a blind man's stare,
I witless, fattened by years of meditation,
handcuffed to my soul could muster one petal
of a sentence: "That is not in my hands."
No one heard the river of my mind become glacier,
no one saw my heart become a glass paperweight
on the fluttering pages of my breath.

He left merely a harmless old man,
the door closed,
the c(l)ock struck twelve,
I stepped back into hell.

In this country you would call him what you call them,
I proved my largesse—we Hindus never, never stoop
as low as our enemy, we swell, our hearts blooming
as fat as this earth, ripe with forgiveness
enough to house two women,
one is a manicured mannequin, plastic perfection,
the other one grows in our bodies,
the dark one, the mad one, the monster one,
the one I've seen come out of myself to tell the world truths with a tongue of fire,
the one who paces my house frothing at the lips,
the one whom every woman carries behind
painted lips and mascara, stilettos and sindoor,
we Indian women sublimate our rage and desire
with the names of Gods and chants and incense,
and our souls buffet in the
serpentine waves of cultures,
our minds a pile of log-dry shards,
we hope, dying, as we chant Rama,

we hope, dying, as we practice Vipassana,
we hope, dying, as we say the zikr,
we hope, we will be liberated by another serpent
docile at the base of our spines,
rise serpent, rise!

And, I showed the face of this poem to the world saying 'us!'
The women in his family cursed and spat and revolted and denied and said,
"Who gave you permission to write of us?" We splintered.
Women turn upon women like scorpions in a basket,
yet we wonder why, why women's true destinies are denied,
I stand alone haggard as a crone the poem in my palm.

*That is not in my hands*

So, let us speak of hands—women's hands, generations of hands,
hands that wash pots with tamarind and mud and feed
drunkards of husbands, hands that pen poetry and fire the guns,
hands that write, harvest paddy with the rising sun,
hands that answer phones at call centers and stave off
rapists' hands of soldiers from both sides of a border,
hands that cook and clean toilets, and are stained with
mehandi, and say goodbye to lovers cleaved from their hearts
because the beats resonate to different religions,
hands that stroke husbands in the night,
and perform puja in the day,
Manu's handmaidens, Sita's clones,
the hands that carry the lamp of tradition,
the hands that light their own pyres,
and clench hospitals beds in childbirths,
the Savitris, bitches, Kalis, yoginis and witches.

This poem is in my hand burning like camphor on my palm,
this poem is the scream of every woman raped,
do not ask me if this is a true poem,
only be singed, our oil feeds the flame.

The flame is singing, the flame is dancing, the flame is shrieking.


*I will not give you sons*

Sir, no Sir, I will not give you sons,
I will abort every male fetus I bear,
I will live to ensure there are no more sons,
I will live to see your bloodline cross over
with you to the other side,
now the blessing from your lips is your execution.

The flame is singing, the flame is dancing, the flame is shrieking.

For the years I walked on thorns backward
from your raised hand, I will not give you sons,
for your madman yell, "I hate her,"
for my parents, midgets in the
monster embrace of Hindu culture,
I will not give you sons,
to make sure you are not resurrected,
for the times I am asked for proof of my pain,
I will not give you sons,
for the brother, father and husband who turned on me,
for the slit on my wrist,
I will not give you sons.

For watching my heart shrivel to
rotting fruit, I will not give you sons,
for spreading the legs of my soul so wide
raped by every bit of male-dominated eternal-truth nonsense,
for accommodating your elephant-sized ego,
and Manu-ized culture in my breast,
for our breasts hot with forgiveness, hate and a community's lips,
No Sir, I will not give you sons.

The flame is singing, the flame is dancing, the flame is shrieking.

For all those fractured women turning on each other,
rich with epithets for men behind their backs,
who point to their head and say, "I hate him,"
and points to their hearts and say, "I love him,"
and walk around dismembered holding their
head in one hand and heart in another,
bleeding and bled, for my eyes burning with Life,
to stay whole, I will not bear you sons.

for turning my marriage into a cremation ground,
where we prey on each other as ghouls,
our goodness reduced to embers,
for being a burning *ghat* burning unquenchable
by any of India's sacred rivers,
for becoming a wound and wounding
when I was once rich as a flower,
I will not give you sons,
my womb will be barren of sons,

The flame is singing, the flame is dancing, the flame is shrieking.

For the dark ones, dark like us,
the spitfire ones, the ones with sparkle and soul-fire,
I will not bear sons, my womb will be dry,
for my daughter to grow as a sunflower rooted in earth,
for her power as woman, man, child, god, goddess,
to watch her undenied, unstoppable by male siblings,
to let her lift herself to the sky with your blood,
to see your sap grow in a woman's body,
to erase the hypocrisy of this family,
my womb will be dry,
I will have daughters dead by female infanticide,
daughters dead by dowry burning,
daughters mutilated by ritual genital cutting,
daughters slicing their wrists,
daughters anemic, anorexic, stunted into size zeros.

I will not bear you sons. The flame is rising.
Onward you will bear my words.

# Raining Elephants

One poet enlightens us about her ovaries and suicide,
another is lofty-visioned, big bells toll and we
are like mice cowering in the crevices of her voice,
one about push-up bras, foxes, communion, origami,
the laws of physics, fences, Pleiades, hats, cherries,
faucets, God, molasses—the plenitude of the universe.

All I want to write about is Love like a wilting
unquenched 16-year-old—its gasping notes, its
fractured limbs, its puckered face, its broken wrist.

And about poetry; that sits like an idol on my countertop,
stalking my attention, sniffing out my suitability
in the middle of the night offering me skeleton hands,
her bony embrace to flesh out.

Chastised by the voluptuous imagination of poets
who know the names of things, and don't say *trees*,
*flowers*. But *belladonna, forsythia, witches hazel*,
and hyphenate oak into its kinds, and dissect the
earth in its latitudes, and break the many rules of poetry
I can't recall, as I never knew in the first place, I ask

myself, why cannot I write about say, this New York
season, a monsoon like thing raining cats, dogs and elephants,
reminding me of another city, 10,000 miles away with women
walking in bunched saris, feet darting about as fish in water.

# Storm

That night Shiva's *hala* dislodged,
thunder snarled, stars rattled
like phlegm in a dying man's throat,
grass knitted black wool,
the branches were epileptic,
lightning flickered like a shaky bulb
in a Hyderabad summer,
the moon slunk off,
the driveway slouched like a somnolent python,
alligator trees climbed upward to an obsidian well,
the drain pipes winced,
the rain galloped on the roof
in my heart, a small scab peeling and bleeding.

In the midst of nun-like houses in rote prayer,
the siding bland as suburban wives' smiles,
these windows a looking glass both ways,
these doors a shut mouth/swallowing secrets.

The storm seeped silent as yeast,
black tar of a water on dark wood
in the bedroom veins.

Termites work from
underneath,
soon the foundation falls
predator life, your work is done.

# Harmony

Her cooking is the honeycomb
that keeps him succulent.
He is seated, King Kong, at the head of the table,
she is unseen, in the kitchen,
sanctified by self-sacrificing labor,
the okra is fried to perfection, has been soaked
in tamarind juice, the sesame seeds pounded and ground
to a paste, poured exactly five minutes before the flame is turned off,
simmering, turned side to side, not too brittle,
supple, gleaming in grainy white coats,
she smugly concedes periphery jobs
to a daughter-in-law who is allowed
to chop and measure, forbidden from
the fine act of cooking in this goddess's kitchen.

There is a hushed silence
in the sanctity of this evening ritual,
the primary steel plate for rice,
the quarter-sized plate for sides like *papadums*,
chutneys and *avakai* and a second vegetable,
a *katori* for the sambar or *kutu*, or *perugu*,
into the meal, this plate might be a repository
for chewed drumsticks, avakai bone, tamarind,
the paraphernalia of supporting herbs
the flotsam and jetsam of ingestible food.

He eats, connoisseur of gastronomy,
she glances sidelong ascertaining his judgement,
every scooped slurped bite is a religious act by a God,
he keeps his face impassive
careful not to spill out too marked an appreciation
keeping the possibility of her pride in check,
doing her a favor, multiplying her virtue.
She understands his face as a farmer knows his soil,
displeased, his face can splinter as drought-land,
as a linguist knows phonemes and syllables—
a twitch, blink, pause, measured stare
and silence are signs signifying things:
a refill of sambar *without* the vegetables/
a refill of sambar *with* the vegetables/
a refill of sambar *with only* the bottle gourd/
the need for raw onions/not enough salt/
he scrutinizes the rotis, tad over burnt, he says,
she is mortified; chastised she hurries to re-make one
more perfect round moon in this perfect harmony.

And I watched exiled from this
soundless solemnity for a decade,
wondering why I could not see the beauty of it.

## General Bazaar

The pent-up scooters, bikes, whatnot,
the mountainous heave of humanity,
needle-like this width is actually a road
when cleared, the hawking life here
was an artery of my childhood,
holding her pallu, winding our way to the goldsmith …
kid brother tagging along, breathless in this flummery of life.

Masterji is still up the steps behind the bag store,
bags pasted on the wall like birds stamped on a tree,
paan-stained teeth, he is apologetic,
of course, the album cover is not ready,
of course, he needs two more days,
of course, I will come again, and again,
to see his decades-worn fingers
among the spindles and color bobbins, bills fluttering
on a wire, ramshackle history of orders taken,
this wizened dealer of female vanities reflected in his perfected eye,
the dull gold or leaf-green? He ponders the
bobbins, colored chess pieces in his eyes.

              My daughter lags behind the sun,
on the other side of night in the maze of school, activities, homework,
trying to remember to call me, filial duty in the hours breaking like
algebra around her, here, I bargain for rhinestone rangolis,
peacock gemmed plaits, paisley giveaway bags,
knowing the real deal's been done,
the child's always the bargain in the whole messy transaction.

# Ordinary

this face,
the day, the killing of children
washing up on shores,
the rape of women, the power race,
the food on the table,
the gargantuan piles of Granny Smiths,
Bartlett pears, Hass avocados, Alaskan cruises,
museums, opera, the onomatopoeia of psychosis;
yoga mats, yoga bandannas, yoga water,
the Mary Janes, stilettos, gold embossed slippers,
zardosi, palazzo pants, Anne Klein,
Nordstrom, winter storms, the travel abroad,
whatever you can afford, whatever's 'mine';

the destination wedding,
the divorce post-wedding, the vows and
semi-vows, love contracted, renewed and voided;
the tabloids of exposé and
celebrities' panty-flashing, Kim Kardashian's
clothes-barely-there-bottomly-flare / Nicki Minaj's
'another day another slay' / and Angelina's adoptions, /
What Caitlyn Jenner Bruce wore to dinner /
(Who's an angel who's a sinner?)
What Amy Winehouse drank before she sank /
and if Britney Spears snores /
(Let's hear moooooore),
Kareena's expecting / Ranbir's grieving / Sonu's on a world tour /
Who's that new thing / who's an angel, who's a whore,
who wears what thong, who's exciting, who's a bore,
ding dong, and a nip, a tuck, and a fuck-and-a-suck

Bieber's doing things you know,
Look at that glow! Selena's crying and growing
up fast, oh gosh oh gosh nothing lasts
but flash bulbs and paparazzi,
and the men from Mars, the women from Venus,
the men from Venus, and the women from Mars,
riding riding their glitzy cars;

our consumption, the hungers, dinners,
outlet malls, tea parties, the things in stores,
the greed for this, the greed for that,
to own all you can own and find that one-eyed cat,
the greed for other countries and the moon
and the young young things want other things too soon;

the slums of ribbed kids with big black eyes,
and our indignation, speedy deliveries via C sections;
"Two orders of MC French fries please!"
Ordinary, theme parties, the shopping, the spending,
the things that eat us like tuition,
aging parents, culture and identity,
find your fat-free solutions or via pill popping
and the Pharm-industry,
Who's that woman crying on her closet floor?
Open the door! Open the door!

The medical surgeries, the transplants,
the man who gave birth to his brother,
the fifty shades of cancer and pleasure,
in your kitchen the display of exotic plants;
ebola, ischemic stroke, COPD, colon cancer,
HIV, diabetes, TB, a new epidemic, aren't you doped?

The Ray-Bans, Gucci, Vera Bradley,
Ordinary is Facebook's five minutes of fame,
Twitter and YouTube,
WhatsApp, Tumblr, plastic boobs,
Snapchat, Instagram, Kik, Pinterest,
Blogs, iPhone selfies, Verizon, Androids, Blackberrys,
God, aren't we merry in our one world nation!
Kindle, chats and e-live your best, clean your desk,
let it go, chill out, learn to flow,
don't come knocking at my door,
I smile, I smile, I've imported my kitchen tiles;

what's in and what's out, the swirl
in your head as you tumble about,
the rabbit's worried time is running out,
breaking news, subscriptions, serial killing,
school shootings, millions of views,
deportations, GOP nominees, Trump
wanted the vacant chair, was he crowned
by Miss Universes in evening gowns?

The talent in reality shows,
the singing voices, the violin prodigies,
magicians, contortionists, the politicians,
blood sucking cops, vampire heroes in movies,
and the day rising with the sun,
and the night dying with the light,
Move on! Put up your fight!

Decomposing bodies in civil wars,
globalism, the books lining shelves in stores,
the UN forces raping and creating other wars,
and fathers raping their daughters,
and brothers booting out their sisters,
You're turning away, why don't you roar?

Rising Kundalini/Isha/Ashtang Yoga,
the peddling of the East in the West,
who's sitting in whose cultural nest?
galactic federation, St Germaine, Maitreya
upanayanams, shamans, bible studies and Bar Mitzvahs,
crystals balls, cartomancy, tarot, Celtic tunes,
I Ching, oils, aromas, feng shui, Theosophy,
pendulums, chalices, runes, crosses, new age lunacy,
the Gods are giving us many boons,
You gotta be linked in? Are you lonely?
See you somewhere sometime soon;

MLK Day, Labor Day, Independence Day,
Hallmark days for this and that,
your dog's vasectomy, the 40th birthday of your cat,
the stripes or the stars on the flags and soldiers
dead on mats or in boxes with crosses on the lids,
Don't flip! Or wake up Sid!

Ordinary the op-eds, and newspapers on and on,
and on World and Business, Reader's Opinions,
Tech and Science, Books and Theater, Education,
Who's alive, who's dead, who's got a gun to his head,
Health, Sports, Arts, Style, Food, Travel and Real Estate,
And knowingly astrology will predict your fate;

Have you tasted fig spread on aged brie? Tasted
the yogis, the bhogis, aghoras and Kundalini;
Please do try! Hurry! Hari! Hurry!

(What's behind the walls in Abu Ghraib?)
Famines, forest fires, oil spills, earthquakes, cyclones,
hurricanes, Nature's hammer hammers sense,
Look up there's the Virgin mourning in a blue dress
soaked with blood, who's telling the truth or a fib?
Do you hear Kali's anklets jingling sounds
as she dances on continents like a cremation ground,
Who's got the loss, who's got the gain?
No matter there's a Jaguar in your garage
even though you're stained.

UFO sightings, pyramids, deep sea creatures—
all ordinary as ordinary can be    don't forget the shows
realer that reality, stars starring in their own obituaries,
the gang rapes, narcotics, the hungry still hungry,
Sep 11, the match fixing, peddling women's bodies,
the sex toys, beauty pageants and the Illuminati,
ceasefires, violations, gay rights, abortion, Top News Stories,
the lonely still lonely shopping in Anthropologie,
(What perfume are you wearing please?)
Shoot or be shot by the jihadis,
It's all for our children's ease;

The whole monster of living and dying,
living and dying daily dying and living,
Stand up and tell me you are alive please!

# Birthday Poem

Every birthday so far—
a fading plinth of genes-hieroglyph,
a batten in the floorwork of memory.

On this day, in the mirror laughing, is a child
in the corridor of my childhood, playing marbles,
she does not think of winning and losing,
and watches the birth of a calf,
a new life clumsily tottering on fours,
on this day I am that calf taking its first step
not knowing the slaughterhouse is around the corner.

On this day I forget—
*Someone always does something for something,*
a temple priest sells you salvation,
on this day I enter the only true temple— the one within,

I know I have dared to be human, it is enough that I know
and the versions of me in others' heads do not haunt me,
on this day supine under the sun, emboldened,
unhurt by my own prehensile abilities
I return home to greet my daughter and meet
a crumpled card with typos that cannot misspell 'Love'.

# Porcupine

*Illness has become my mate, bound by ties of blood and nerves and bone, and I hold with it long secret conversations.*

—Kamala Das, *My Story* (p. 212)


Where does she hide,

    the one who sends black meteors in the canvas of my skin?

I was born a girl I suppose, I've now become a porcupine,

all that touches me pricks, all that I touch is pricked.

Burning effigy in a desert I don't stop burning.

Iceberg. I am frozen. I don't thaw.


I digest nothing        I roam black tunnels at night,


I am a dart board        unskinned animal salted,

    dervish-vertigo prays often in my head.


And other such creatures:

aposematic   tiger moth   cuttlefish   pitohuis: what I ingest, I emit,

I grow quills, I am toxic, my skin is prickled leaves,

blue-ringed     blue-throated     blue-bruise planet,

        I become yellow when approached,

Crown-of-thorn starfish in royal purple my spines are sharp.

        I am an ecosystem of pain.

Neck turning on creaking hinges,

muscle-fibers are wood,

diaphanous jellyfish     I sting myself     a glance can tear my skin.

A s a k n i f e  s c r a p i n g b r e a d a n d  c r u m  b l i n g,
I am the knife, the bread and the crumbling crumbs,

     not veins but rope,

     not skin but shroud,

      my days are a sunset to sunset,


fibro  m y a l g i a
     thoughts sizzle apart like weak batter on a pan.


Will I ever emerge through a wormhole

            crowned with stars?

# Bridges

Unbridge the latitudes that arise from hate,
Erase the deep grooved-longitudes of an old earth,
We are here, we do not come to stay,
The earth is round to some, flat to some,
Some come to do, some to undo,
Some bridges are breaking from too much load,
Let our steps be the flight of doves,
Let our roads be incense.

You and I are guests, this planet belongs to children,
Where are the dinosaurs that lorded the earth?
The builder of the pyramids, temples and hanging gardens?
What if I told you this earth is one bolt in a bridge
whose masonry we cannot fathom?
Have we not felt the unseen caissons holding this universe?

The original destiny of the continents was a handshake,
We come adrift in error and end in sky, earth or water.
Let us like the War-Khasi grow bridges organically
root in earth, thwart gravity, rise majestically from heart to heart.

Let us offer our children our wisdom not our greed.
Let us ask today, tomorrow and every day,
"Have I thawed at least one hard sinew in my heart?
Am I lighter when I reach the other side?"

# Simple Equations in the Niyogi Worldview

Braided hair,
oiled,
unexciting,
= chaste
= Virtuous.

Jean,
hair-halo,
wild
= Wanton.

Wanton
= promiscuous, immoral, immodest, indecent, shameless,
   loose, impure, lustful, whorish and disreputable.
= uncultured
= Non-Brahmin
= Non-marriageable.

# Witch

*Layers of ladyfingers soaked in mocha latte,*
*layered with whipped cream, cranberry jam, ganache,*
What does this mean in a household teetering like Jell-O?
This random Facebook post, a leaf byte falling
to make you salivate, the offerings on someone's table,
while a child's heart's ripped as butterfly wings,
one mother, one father, *Child, my child!* I cry,
her mind's shaky-flaky pastry crumbling,
my guilt is cotton-stuffing on a scab,
a Dettol singe in a house of torn-ligament hours.

Daughter of mine, I am bleeding too as I bleed you,
What are my offerings to you?
My heart marinated mango in mustard and chilies
on our less-than-white, less-than-black skin,
*kali mirch* soaking into apples, cardamom-spiced whipped cream,
the avoidance of eye-to-eye, unblended condiments of conversation,
another failed morning at the threshold.

I do not want to be that mother flying, flying furiously on my broom,
or that one who is found
    under the house,
       after a house flies and crashes,
       and you child are Dorothy so befuddled,
       a grown-up in a gingham dress.

# I Can't/Won't Write Like a White Male Poet

Hold up the onion skin of your poetry
to the light,
You are nothing,
A drum roll,
With no procession.

What is your flag?
But a terrain of occupation,
A McDonald poetry,
Your epic is not long,
Birthed through size zero thighs,
Your gluten free poetry.

You try hard to be real,
Toilet poetry of confessions,
Platitudes masquerading as wisdom,
Wheezing voice with no bass,
Oh! Take off your mask!
Your invented sorrow!

Poetry of constipation,
Forced breath,
Hemorrhaging lines,
Seething bloodless,
Devoid of sap.

Where I come from,
We are burned,
Write with a thousand hands,
We are oiled,
Scarred,
Scathed,
And speak with a tongue 10,000 centuries long,
You were in diapers conjuring Freud's architecture,
When we mapped the serpentine coils of the soul

No, I am not pressing the feet of history,
I watch over history with 1,000 hoods,
I live with a pantheon of Gods,
I dare to render the one into many,
We churn oceans,
Drink immortality,
Hold poison in our throats,
Ride lions as our steeds,
We are not protected in the belly
of some large fish cowering in safety,
We are the waters that hold the fish,
We carry bloodied axes and raze demons,
Hold the world on our amphibian backs.

We come like a tornado over your borders,
Exchange your God for our Gods,

You've punctured the world with your wounds,
Punctuated the stories with your stakings,
My poetry does not come down the
slides of Schlitterbahn with mint breath.

Go find Whitman's pen,
Lincoln's hat,
Visit Mary Oliver in the woods,
Go next door,
Visit Paz and Neruda,
Leave your cities,
Set your country on fire,
Lament like Darwish,
Mourn like Amichai,
Be imprisoned like Hikmet,
Get shot like that young black boy,
Move out of your cities,
Cross the Atlantic,
Burn your MFA degrees,
Torch the wholesale voice of your poems,
Allow poetry to come in,
Don't go Dutch in a restaurant,
Don't tell me to go home,
Own your garbage,
Stop marketing,
Know your neighbors,
Don't make your charity tax deductible,
Dismantle the industry of poetry,
Stop stealing,
Don't write ghazals (you can't),
Or Haikus (you can't),
Stop trivializing everything with 'OK' and 'Great!'

Write a poem,
Not in your favorite place,
Not in your B&N hardbound journal,
Not with your Schaeffer pen,
Don't organize your binders,
or use gel pens or post its,
The world is burning with the torch you lit,
Write your poems
On the ticket stubs of history like me,
Open borders that matter,
Then, I'll write a poem like you.

# A Lot of Light Because It Was Like a Concert

So much breaking news everybody is broken,
Who wakes up whole when the sun rises?
Let me know, learn to twist your tongue in new names
to count history's footsteps: Tenancingo/
Abdelhamid Abaaoud/ Aulnay-sous-Bois/
Hasna Ait Boulahcen/Bataclan/Bernard Cazeneuve.
Know boys will be boys and the clan is the clan,
And we will strengthen our borders to keep the madness in,
And Justin Bieber can end a show after one song,
And Karla is raped 43,200 times four years long,
And who has the true religion in this gallimaufry?
Explain it any way you can—our earth, turquoise marble in
a pristine mind coming undone, perhaps
the clash between yin and yang, the apogee and perigee of sin,
While the officials take their papillary prints and
some are sure someone measures the soul's thumbprint,
And someone can say of carnage:
"And a lot of light because it was like a concert."

Go figure that!

The captain of the commandos, who wanted to be known only as Jeremy, told NBC News he
    entered the theater to find several hundreds of people lying motionless on the floor, not
    making a sound. "Tons of blood everywhere. No sound. Nobody was screaming… and a lot
    of light because it was like a concert." CNN NEWS, Fri November 20, 2015
Tenancingo: Mexican city where girls are raised to be prostitutes.
Abdelhamid Abaaoud: male suicide bomber, Paris attacks, November 2015
Aulnay-sous-Bois: hometown of Hasna, female suicide bomber.
Hasna Ait Boulahcen: female suicide bomber, Paris attacks, November 2015
Salah Abdeslam: male bomber, Paris attacks, November 2015
Bernard Cazeneuve: French interior minister
Bataclan: concert hall where attack occurred.
Karla: human trafficking victim

## In This Room

In this room
the hours are stars
I count them.

Precious, their soft light
is a mirror
I see a woman

Who sees the hours are stars
not the darkness
on which the hours grow.

In the mirror she is smiling
and as calm as
a finger tracing the stars.

The walls are angel wings
They help her fly.

She is with the stars now,
or the hours, call them anything,
today, they shed light.

## I Am Not a bed

to carry the weight of history's backside.
I am not a chair for you to sag the buttocks of traditions,
I am not a table to lay your wares on,
Not even that bookshelf to place your stories,
No, not that curio to display your gains in the world,
And not the kitchen sink to rinse your shame,
Not your wall listening to your heroic stories,
Not the curtains hiding your guilt.
Not the window to close out the air, the sun, the moon,
I am not your ladle to measure your inadequacies,
Not your Italian tiles to shine …
I am not your house to gather your ghosts.

See that open door

       into the world, I am that,

        Gone.

## Walls

There is no perfume of fear
in these walls.
What color is this air?
If I say rose,
rose becomes shroud,
and if I say sunflower
its head will droop
with the setting sun.

The stars do not shine here giddily
or the vertigo of ellipsis,
or the coffin of night
or the hysterics of the sun.

These walls are not the holes between bars.

What is this room
where a woman sleeps
without a flushed cheek
or labored heart?

# Reading the South American Poets

Orchard of sounds, pens tipped with fire,
throats warm with poetry, poems moist
with honey, poems of molten lava, lines
like swills of the flamenco, poems buoyant
with yeast, poems rising, poems of conquest,
exile, ferment of politics, savage lands,
poems of myth—clash of armor, ardor
and crumbling walls. Poems like protection
from winds, like rivers coming full circle,
like oracle, bird song, sundial and shapes of light.
Poetry that comes like wind in tunnels,
rises like steeples and mountains and falls like
bones of water, buxom flesh of avocado
poetry like eyes that see, and
the gnashing of teeth, black holes, wells and mirrors,
war bugles and the earth's sweat and toil.

Poems like scented milk, thighs of a woman
like orgasms, like crosses, poems wet with
longing. Succulent oranges, I taste your
heat, longing, your fervor, your fever, your
earth, your sky, your root, your bread,
your love, your flag, your blood, you.

# Poetry in Spicy Mango Gravy

*Ingredients:*

A.
½ ripe yellow mango
6 tbsp old memories
3 tbsp fresh metaphors
2 fresh images, conceited and coy
1 bunch nostalgia, chopped
2 tsp alliteration
2 grated familial roots

B.
½ cup concrete language
3 tbsp abstractions

C.
1 tbsp poetic license (or more by taste)
1 tbsp risk
1-2 tsp cultural identity (spice powder)
8 ounces sensory details

D.
A selection of figures of speech

*Procedure:*

Place ingredients A in a food processor and blend for a minute.

Add in B & D: concrete language, abstractions and figures of speech;
blend for 30 secs.

You may form it into a symbol if you are tempted to.

Heat poetic license in kadai, wok or pan.

Pour in the above mixture and cook in poetic license for 5–10 mins.

Add risk to taste requirement.

Add the cultural identity powder.

Stir.

Next, add figures of speech and sensory details, cook over medium heat
for 2–3 mins or until soaked, moist and dissolved.

They must make a perfect poem with suggestive power, all pieces perfectly
blended.

Avoid cultural appropriation.

Garnish with roasted or lightly fried title.

Serve with any respectable journal or online magazine.

# Twilight

Blue orchid sky
      I pluck you,
   adorn my hair.

My hair becomes a river
murmuring ink-stained stream.

Papaya sun, from this window
      I dip my hands in you.

My ochre-stained fingertips
are keys to open hidden cities.

Blue iris, red pupil
      looking back at me.
   I fly into your dreams.

My dreams rained with you.

## Shards

I was born in a field of shards; their names

deep,

too deep to find. I know them all, know their names.

                        Sshh.
        I want to sacrifice all names in
sacrificial pyres …                wear
                a gown of flame.


In the coffin of the night the eyeballs of
                        stars glimmer with a losing light.

I dreamt of horses. And my daughter running;
                and I running, and my husband running; and
there was one wild horse that
                came for us. I remember the
running. How like an arrow she flew—
my daughter; and I
boled on awkward and turned into a side gate.

I awoke. The dream
                was a shard of bigger shard


I awoke a bird in a golden cage, gold

around me gold and glass and the
sun pouring its undulating crochet on the walls I
am hypnotized by glass and light shadow
and trees, and the sun's deceptions of beauty.

I awake. I
am a
ray of
diss
olving
light, my
part
icles float
ing in the
house,
at night I am a moon
beam and

a leaf on
a tree embroidering the sky…

Like logs of wood I lie scattered in the forest of the house.

[Good morning doctor. This morning, when I awoke there was a
twitch in my right eye, and a twitch in my left arm; *like sparrows
saying farewell before they become extinct* … my hands were burning and
deep in my right palm *an island congealed;* a nerve burned *brightly like
a torch,* my finger joints are very stiff *like fossils from another age.* Yes
doctor, the neck is stiff too, trying to do some gentle yoga. C5, C6 …
*clicked and clacked, frozen like a can lid refusing to open,* yes, yes, will set
up physiotherapy appointments, no, not yet. Have increased insulin
intake, no, no, won't taper down without telling you, please call
insurance for coverage verification.]

this body a jigsaw puzzle breaking apart …

Glass walls shatter vases shatter, I take
the glass with me to each realm I live in; and the heart icicle is cracking

in a slaughterhouse

*Am I a goddess, maybe I could be a goddess, maybe I can be alive. Let me chant Lalitha on Fridays, add on Khadgamala and Sri Vidya, in the evenings Maha Mrutyunjaya and at night Shirdi Baba Parayanam. Let me be a good Niyogi woman, let me be sanctified, let me learn the art of living and breathing …*

> *Do you think someone's coming on a horse for you?*
> *Make us happy, make yourself happy.*
> *Be like us. Be a good daughter.*
> *You meditate. You should not get hurt anymore.*
> *You need to prove yourself to our family.*
> *You need to be like us, like our family.*
> *Who asked you to stand up for us?*
> *We hate you.*
> *Coward.*
> *Uncultured.*
> *Crack.*
> *You should not be so honest.*
> *You think you are a poet but you are a crack.*
> *Be practical.*
> *Men are easy to manage. All they need is sex and food.*
> *Manage your husband.*
> *Please your husband.*
> *Do not come to me with your problems.*
> *As long as people are good to me, I don't care what they do to you.*
> *Do you think you are a great poet?*
> *Do you think you are a great Sufi?*
> *Get your head out of the clouds.*

I enter pyramids made of shards of poems.

I enter home—tomb—womb.

# Darbar of Frogs

In the darbar of frogs, the green amphibians sipped fragrant nectar with honey from garish silver goblets seated on thrones engraved with the words 'Sanatana Dharma'. Their slimy toxic skin perspired in the heat. Their stewards waved fans made of the soft silky mane of horses. The cushions were plump purple velvet stuffed with swan feathers. "The swan!" the messenger announced, blowing his conch accompanied by kettle drums.

One hundred pairs of beady eyes fixed the swan who arrived pale and glistening. She was a new bride. "Not too white," a she-frog whispered, shaking her head in disapproval, her bulging eyes, bulging even more.

"But we received a high bid instead," the mother-in-law sniffed, a small smile on her face as she showed off a pair of 22-carat-gold bangles studded with diamonds to her sister. "There is no one like my prince," she said, "no girl would be good enough for him anyway, so we compensate in other ways."

The heavens had decided the swan be married to a handsome frog, it was deemed a match made in heaven. The astrologers had tallied the compatibility points to an astonishing 47 out of 50, a match made in heaven to the nod of Rahu and Ketu; Saturn leerily smiled. His net was cast.

"Hi!" said the swan.

"She said, die! Did you hear that? She wants us dead." They looked at each other nodding convinced. "She is bad! Bad! Bad! Bad!" echoed in the hall.

"Does she not know she has to croak three times to greet us. How westernized she is. Uncultured!"

"She's a swan! She's bad!"

"She has feathers! She's bad!

"She is fairer than us! She is bad!"

"She sings swan songs! She is bad!"

"Now she sits! She is bad!"

"Now she stands! She is bad!"

"She is alive!"

"Bad! Bad! Bad!"

"Hi. What am I on trial for?" the swan said, confused. They ignored what she said, adjusting their *pallus* on their head.

"We are amphibians. We have two lives. We will finish you as a swan and resurrect you as a frog."

"But I am a swan," she said, bewildered. "I know I am a swan. And must remain a swan."

"We are here to make you a frog," they said resolutely.

She noticed her sisters, best friends, brothers, husband, neighbors, aunts, uncles, cousins, father, mother, teachers, gurus, ex-boyfriends knotted alongside her in-laws. They had conjoined as a family bowing and greeting one another. Her in-laws wore aluminum foil crowns convinced they would pass off as silver. Her parents dipped deep to the ground to keep second rank. The penises of all the male frogs rode high like those ropes in the rope-trick of sadhus. And her family, though they were swans, incredulously looked like frogs now. They were turning color and their wings grew shorter and eyes distilled to reflect the undercurrent hate seeping in from a distant past. The women were darkening to a depper hue of green with envy. They all looked ready to feast, their sticky tongues darted in and out of their mouths as they looked at the swan.

"We know how, give us your crystal heart!" The swan handed over her heart to the frogs without hesitating, trusting this was normal. Her mother had shopped for silver-handle hammers for the occasion. They each proceeded to hammer her heart till it was a smashed vase of smithereens reflecting light in crisscross patterns. The light illumined the space around her in strange patterns not seen before. The frogs were not happy that there was still light radiating from her heart.

"Yes, yes," her father was saying to her father-in-law, "she must give up her swansongs if her husband wants it. It is her duty." Her father was growing smaller and smaller each moment, while her father-in-law loomed like Aladdin's genie. Her father-in-law smiled pompously and they both nodded with well-worn wisdom. "Yes," he said, croaking stiffly, "it is her duty, this is how it was done and will be done, she must learn to belch, burp, squelch like us, learn to flick a tongue and catch flies all day. What will we do with her swan songs?" he added dismissively, and stretched out his goblet for a refill. "Yes, yes," said the elder brother-in-law, imitating his father's stance, "she must prove herself to us." All the women looked at each other smirking and sharing secret smiles. She could hear one brother's whiny nasal voices like a twang in the chorus. The boyfriends tittered whispering to each other, "I chased her till she chased me." "She was chaste and desirable till I saw her desire me too. Chee chee." Their wives were seated behind them in purdah.

"We'll pluck her feathers now to make her a frog." They nodded unanimously. The astrologers looked thoughtful making many calculations in their notebooks. "It is time," they nodded agreeably. The priests cleared their throats and began to recite Sanskrit slokas. Manu, the head priest, was a very busy frog these days. He had hundreds of skinning-the-swan events to officiate. His round belly bobbed about if he moved. In between, he paused to answer his cell phone, his red eyes gleaming at the mentioned officiating fees, his underlings keeping the chanting uninterrupted, obsequiously at his side.

It was an eternal trial. They plucked her feathers, one by one—she screamed, she wailed her swansongs, then stuttered them, till they devolved to croaks and four-lettered words. Her language became guttural. I am becoming a frog, she thought aghast. She looked in a mirror and saw two reflections, a swan and a frog. Who am I? she thought bewildered. Sometimes in the mirror there was another mirror and within that mirror another, a procession of mirrors reflecting unknown faces that were supposed to be hers, faces fashioned in features by the words of others.

The brother with the whiny voice declared, "How impious is her language, she has none of our culture. Good women don't use language like this," beaming in approval at his wife who was mouthing the *Vishnusahasranamam* in a Kanjeevaram sari. He sent his apologies for his sister's behavior to the in-laws often and invited them to his house for meals which his wife served traditionally on banana leaves, her eyes averted modestly. He presided graciously serving them with just enough deference. They were pleased that he agreed she had to bear the feather-plucking stoically in silence. It was disrespectful to protest, it sullied their honor, and besmirched the great tradition they all came from.

She tearfully turned to her parents, "It hurts!" Her father said, wisdom furrowing his brow, "You are imagining! You are not in pain. All is maya. It is your karma. Bear it. If you cannot bear it, ignore it." He closed his eyes and was mostly supine on the bed. He had more important things to thinks about like the possibility that Abraham was actually Telugu. After all, everything was sourced in or from India. One day they would also realize that Solomon's temple was in Dwaraka. He was irritated. He was not the kind of man who asked for much as long as he got what was due to him, he was a gentleman, nothing short of a yogi—he didn't complain about the food his wife served, or the way she folded his clothes, or the temperature of the water she heated for his bath. He was a peaceful man; he minded his own business not his daughter's. The effort it would take him to get off the couch and grow a spine. It was too much work at his age.

Her mother was neurotically occupied with pleasing all she could with her good acts in society. She kept very busy so she did not have to think. She forgot all her feathers had been plucked too and the swan was her daughter. Like all good mothers, she had beaten down the swan in her childhood to make sure she didn't get a swollen head later on and become too fine a swan. It was for her own good. Or worse still, how could she be outshined by her daughter?

When she turned to her husband for help, he said, "I cannot be disloyal to my own. Deal with it." He loved the frogs of his family. They seemed to croak so beautifully in unison but now they seemed discordant to him. He hated that he had to see it differently. Especially his mother who was the most beautiful of them all—a queen to whom one must bow—didn't seem so beautiful anymore. He saw that they were not gold, just toads that ate other frogs. He hated that he had to see the world differently and grow up. He gave the swan the best vegetation to eat, a big car, a house and Gucci perfumes to shut her up. He was secretly afraid of her as he knew swans ate frogs. His unvoiced secret was that he wanted her to be a frog without looking like one. He became unforgiving and yet magnanimously supported all that she aspired to do with her hemorrhaging wings. What a good husband am I, he thought puffing out his frog chest incrementally over time.

It was an open house this darbar. The swan grew bald, pink and paler, the blood flowed on the darbar floor. No one seemed to notice they were wading in a river of blood; the chairs floated, wetting their little dangling legs. They distractedly wiped off droplets of blood. Slowly, her family, extended family, her married-into-family exited her life one by one, shutting their ears to keep out the swan's guttural sounds; they exiled her. Her sisters, and she-cousins were delighted that she had finally become as bad as they knew she was. It made them feel good about themselves. They even insisted on hearing her songs and speech as guttural even when they were not. The swan lived alone for a long time with the reflections in the mirror to keep her company. She noticed, miraculously, it seemed like her feathers never wholly disappeared. The more they plucked, more sprouted. She lived in pain but sprouted quills to write her songs.

And one day, the swan looked in the mirror and saw only one reflection— hers. Just like that, one day it happened. She'd also learnt to live alone for so long she became unafraid of anything. And her voice came back stronger and sweeter than ever.

She lifted up her stripped wings and flew away. It was a wobbly flight. But flight.

In the red silence below no one cared. Outside, were more swans on trial— daughters, sisters and mothers. There was plenty to be occupied with for a long time.

# Erasure

Like leaves, like chameleons, her poems. The color, peeling a little differently, sometimes like hibiscus, something like mangoes, leaking juices, staining pages. She, chasing herself. The poems were butterflies in the sun. Her net caught none. They left like swallows, like bats, like penguins. They left unafraid of homelessness.

When they left, she was orphaned. She was a star fallen from the apron of the mother, fallen like a song joining the void of her memories hovering on the blush of the rose.

She met her poems in the desert behind her eyes. They had heard the call of the wilderness. Some greeted her cold-eyed, filled with a sense of abandonment and accusation, to be so exposed! Some were blindfolded, some like lanterns, always a confusion of joy and sorrow, wisdom and unknowing. Some greeted her, bowed, curtsied, shook hands, mumbled or said *adaab* or *namaste*. Others whirled like dervishes; and some left a cold blanch on her cheek. Others were re-named so strangely they were bewildered, mumbling distracted, begging to be claimed. Soon her poems, a silent kingdom spreading like an ink stain on the earth's eye. Like a ghost she enters them, erased gradually, seeking what the great poets sought.

"Do not seek to follow in the footsteps of the wise; seek what they sought."
— Matsuo Bashō

# Enough!

People let us say it.

Bring back our caged children to a field of sunflowers,
open our land to people as we would our palms
to catch a raindrop,
bring back Aylan in blue shorts
washed up as a fish, snuggled in sand,
let us not say again: he did not make it,
let children not have to tell their stories.

Let us bring back Gulsoma, seven years old,
oil her back scarred like a cluster of sardines,
let us hear her laughter before she was married,
let Malala not be shot in the head, let Karla
not have to say 43,200 raped.

And bring back Asifa Bano's rosy cheeks and chirping,
let her bring back goats bare-footed,
and roast warm chestnuts on a humble fire,
let her eight-year-old legs not be parted brutally for
things other than what children do,
and bring back all the murdered girl infants
still as stone swaddled in earth.

And the police/traffickers/abductors/
mothers/fathers/sisters/brothers
who kill/sell/abuse/rape/shoot their own,
let us hang them as rotting fruit from trees.

And people, we who know too much with our tentacles of knowing
like octopus with many eyes, how much of knowing do we need,
before we say it?

## Not Enough

For the truth is, I have not traced
a face longingly as an embroiderer
traces the outline of a flower,
I have sublimated love to nameless abstracts—God,
humanity, and such—engulfed them all
in a cavernous mother's heart,
I am air loving air.

And to this heart, confession box too which it is:
I say: *this is not enough.*

How poets write! How persimmons swell on silk,
and a nightingale sings from the branches to dulled senses,
the tenderness that must come from the lessons of love,
the knowledge of the fruit, of aching coupling,
wanting imperfect sand dunes of one certain body,
human breath from the cave of a mouth,
a voice that is a bell in the bones
a presence the taste of cardamom chai,
the hours like wild horses,
and a day ripening to the color of crushed cherries;
to long for the smell of hair like cloves, rain or camphor,
to want fingers to make music in hair.

That kind of love, I have not known
lost in the civility of traditions wrapping around me
five-and-a-half times,
I have been loved for civil things,
it has left me dry as a funeral log,
instead, my poems set off as tremulous paper boats
in Indian monsoon puddles          this is second best.

And this is as confessional as I will get
because my blood is not of birth and resurrection
but of a goddess who wears a garland of skulls living in the world.

# On Turning Fifty

I give a million thanks today
        for the sun,
for the dancing paisley of the breeze,
           the broken leases of God's unkept promises,
        the crochet shadows of the trees,
                I think it, I thunk it, I thank it.

for the ink in this pen,     my lifelong companion,
        for the poems these words become,
           for the wisdom in simple rhymes,
for the ones who loved me    for the ones who did not, mocked and rocked,
           for cuckoo clocks that did not chime,
and the ones who hounded me from their hearth,
        for the ones who gave me birth,
for the petty bazaars in which I was sold,
        for this or that, for some petty price,

                I think it, I thunk it, I thank it,
                  I rise.

And the ones who called me names,
        or propelled me on the road to fame,
        or thought I'd be bought,

        I think it, I thunk it, I thank it.

I am not the ocean on many days,
        just a wave falling in, in, in,
and the sky seems a shroud of sin,
        and not the garment of his robe,
        I think it, I thunk it, I thank it.

And on some days, I leap, I surge,
and laughter is a happy dirge,
I know I am all that flows,
and a wrinkle's just a crease of time,
and I am ready for Death if he comes through the door,

I admit, I've played the fool
amidst too many wise men,
and I am a simpleton who loves way beyond her ken,
I think it, I thunk it, I thank it,
I'm lit.

As a candle holding still in a tornado,
I can let it all go.

This life, this life!
the blessings are blows,
I quietly row on the foam of days,
the blows are blessings,
and yet I'll say,
even though the roses have thorns
and thorns have roses unborn,

I think it, I thunk it, I thank it,
I don't quit.

I've been young and told I was centuries old,
I am old now and growing young,
there are lilies blooming on days of dung,
for those unsung heroes
and unqualified imposters,
and the doves of war, and the doves of peace,
crisp pastel linen sheets,
I think it, I thunk it, I thank it,

For this body,
        this body a matrix of pain,
      mostly, a jigsaw coming apart,
          like petals falling from a flower,
     and still, and still, it holds my beating heart,
           and saints have come in the sepulcher of the night,
        held out palms like lamps of light,
            for that alone,
                I think it, I thunk it, I thank it.

I thank the crosses that I bear,
        the glistening moist breakfast pear,
nothing is what it ever seems,
    We are awake in someone's crumbling dream.

      Oh! I laugh and laugh and laugh at it all,
        I am an oyster with a hidden pearl,
         the mumble, the jumble, the rumble, the tumble,
            the bumble of it all,
        the saints are sinners,
        the sinners are winners,
        I watch the phantom of the play with a smile and cry,
          the years have rolled by as marbles,
         they take all I have, will have or had,
             I think it, I thunk it, I thank it,
         thank His incomprehensible wit,
        as he carelessly throws our lives as darts,
        and we tumble about in fits and starts.

      I'm still walking on my feet free,
         freer than the breeze,
            I can think it, I thunk it, I thank it.

There's always been a Hand
    within the many hands that shake my hand,
        hands that are swords or sweet words or new roads,
            and that hand is her,
            and that hand is him,
      Finally, I know
                        I can think it, I thunk it, I thank it,
    I could go today      without regret,
      I'll go laughing every bit,
                        I can think it, I thunk it, I thank it,
for I breathe finally breaths without tears,
      turning fifty, I turn without fear.

# The Repetition of It in Sri Lanka, and Elsewhere

Every day I lose a part of me,
sprinkled about with bodies in some country,
like charred logs of wood we lie,
my intestines become smoke howling in the sky.

I am a scream from a raped woman's throat,
I am washed up on some shore without a shoe,
I am a child living in a house of wire,
a fish suffocating in water,
a bird that cannot fly.

I move about without fingers on some days,
some days without a head,
and always the heart hangs by a thread,
not sure whom or what to pump for
I join the living dead.

I am Hindu, I wear orange,
I am Muslim, I wear green,
I am a nun cloistered in a forgotten dream,
I am a man loving a woman,
A woman loving a woman,
A woman loving a man,
And whatever color I wear or whatever prayer I say,
Whomever I love or lie with,
'the other' will torch me till I am bone.
I join the living dead as stone.

## Adam Walking Backward

The season of certainties is past,
the earth slips like an eel,
hard to grasp, neither science comforts
nor religion nor social awareness.
There *was* a tiger, a gorilla, a leopard,
there *was* a bird, there *was* Man, there *was* a child,
we will say soon, this mess,
this diurnal dirge of Nature,
this was a planet once.

In the kaleidoscope shifts of the earth's destiny,
too late we write poems, treat the earth as a
rosary bead with sanctity. "Too late, too late,"
we know this is the heartbeat,
like "caw caw," in the sky as the Hawaiian crow-call faded.

The green recedes like a hairline,
blue, blue is our future.  And the rains
come like an ominous doorbell. And the fire
comes like a lion devouring, and the earth's despaired-rumble
in her belly. Under muted breath, Hindus mutter *pralaya*,
a continent slips through an orifice,
glaciers slide innocently into the sea like a friendly
handshake, and we leave the seventh cause of
climate change                           nameless.

Arabian owl, Seychelle parakeet,
New Zealand quail, ivory-billed woodpecker,
skunk duck, passenger pigeon—where are the birds?
The feathered glory of flight?
Disappearing names knelled in the cave of history
like arcane Sanskrit chants; we cremate ourselves,
species by species, piece-by-piece,
this is Adam walking backward, taking his
names back, giving back the apple to Eve,
*The lands shall be crisscrossed with a spider's web.*

# Method of Handwashing

Use soap and running water
Rub your hands vigorously
Wash all surfaces, including
Back of hands
Wrists
Between fingers
Under fingernails
Rinse well
Dry hands with paper towel
Turn off the water using a paper towel,

Then, with bare hands,
dirty your soul in Abu Ghraib.

# Boomerang

We are boomeranged
   in the lattice of destiny by a deft hand,
      the years a burning bush,
         a life—pilgrimage and sacked city—
            we are arched to the uneven spin
               bending hardness, curving by cultural burn
                  and—retrieved from flight to the source.

                 You gifted me this metaphor.
                 I was six when I tasted the sweet cream of childhood
              in your croissant-shaped boundaries,
           —and still didn't know our totemic links
          —that you too stepped off a landmass—
       and before that—we—all of we—dreaming—
     stepped out of the dreaming
   as a nascent blue globe—eyeball of god
watching its own birth and decay—

Boomerangs have a special curved shape and two or more wings that spin to create
   unbalanced aerodynamic forces. These forces —called 'lift' — cause the boomerang's path to
   curve in an elliptical shape, so that it will return to the thrower when thrown correctly.

# On the Broken Line

And the days can stream
like a row of black piano keys,
make a kind of music with no relief,
and upon us, a quiet despair
staples the days.

Our patina dreams, and our prayers
come, but come as shadows of light,
a quiet shriek, black flags on the
heart's terrain,
        hyena headlines.

        We are devoured daily,
and in this palimpsest of pain,
we soon forget our sighs reach the heavens,
and what seems all too late,

suddenly,
on the broken line,
        a new poem begins
to write itself,
and this, we call Grace.

WE

# Women Speak

*for us*

Even if you feel your days are held in place
with safety pins,
and you are unbuttoned by life daily,

harangue the stars with your voices,
they cannot be trusted,

speak!
Women.

# Naming

*for Jyoti, Delhi rape survivor*

*We want the world to know her real name. My daughter didn't do anything wrong, she died while protecting herself. I am proud of her. Revealing her name will give courage to other women who have survived these attacks. They will find strength from my daughter.*
                    —Father of Jyoti, Delhi rape case, 2012 BBC Hindi.


She was returning home from watching *Life of Pi*,
the hero lived to tell the tale
in a boat shared with animals … was this a sign from
fate? Her journey in a bus with predators:

                    six men falling
                                    upon her like hyenas,
                    a wheel jack handle and metal rod plunged
in her private parts, the intestines ripped out,
in a moving bus circumambulating Munirka,
bite marks across her body … death in a Singapore hospital.

Her mother's eyes were dark charcoal, unspilled lakes,
*She died but we die every day … Kudrat bhi ne hamare saath nahin diya*


                    When the dots finally connected they were black,
black gags, gnashes across their mouths, black dressed,
the women gathered in India Gate, Raisina Hill,
the drum beat of marching feet in cities spelt *Justice* …

                    women as petroleum, she the wick
                              keeping the flame burning.

If this day is a fruit, it is a papaya, with a black heart
in the gaudy gold of a nation; if a flower, the frangapani,
its milky sap blistering a nation's veins; if a fish, *vaam*,
as her intestines like eels on the bus floor;
if a tree, the tamarind souring the breath of India.

And if a name: Jyoti
emerging like a lion from a cave,
whisking the world like a tornado,
Enough!

By Indian law a rape victim's name is not published. The victim was given the name Nirbhaya
in the media.
*Kudrat bhi ne hamare saath nahin diya*: Even God was not on our side.

# Blue Was Your Landscape

*for Meera Bai*

You tinted the desert blue with a glance,
Twilight with its storm-heavy clouds
hid in your eyes as his signature,
When you slept the blue sky plunged into you.

Your destiny, blue,
Your mind, heart, blue waters,

Your heart so chiseled it was a flute of holes
spilling a name,
A name dragging you out of every comfort:
body, desire, mind, sex, husband, kingdom, family,
except your songs
falling from blue lips
swaying your feet in common alleys
with God-drunk inebriates.

Leading you from Kutch to Brindavan to Dwaraka,
Hypnotized, you followed
a ribbon of longing,
And he is silent, his work done.

And      we, Meera?
Obliterated in your stinging piety,
Our bodies burning for more things than God.

# Video et Taceo

*for Anne Boleyn*

Listen, Anne.

The light is growing faint in the talons of time,
There, in a pulpit of imagined sin,
In the eyelid of the stars you are silent.

Silent, the blood-heat.
Silent, the falconry of love.
Silent, the lute of promises.
Crocuses of dust!

Knelled, gutted, interred,
Unheaded daisy,
Bottle-less cork,
Perfume-less rose,
Your puppet-years beheaded.

The earth set you spinning,
The stone took you in,
The leaves are guessing your whereabouts.

We hear the murmuring of fear
in this lake of silence,
spindles of air prick the heart.

Here, you lie in the swaddling of stone,
Dreaming of glinting fields of axe blades
Praying with a tongue of ash,
Green castles are distant,
Your color reigns.

# Joysmos

*for Magda Carneci and Ruxandra Cesereanu*

*'A reader will read us one day' from the poem 'A Vast Reader'*

These poems you *write  write to*  by which you tear scratch
carve delineate the universe  on your terms this tug-of-war with
the world        your right        your triumph
your big                    gulps of air        to live      to breathe
to be        my sisters-in-arms,

I am warmed in my bed now, I salute your poems
outside the dull-leaved oaks like ancient alligators
climbing to the sky, you bursting open the seams of words
as yellow pollen scatters in the air this very moment

outside my window,

I admit I do not know the trees or flowers in your country,
but here *morning glory, basket flower, coreopsis*
are shrill announcements calling my attention,

                                    name us! they cry aloud,

in my bed now asking a thousand questions        the names
of your trees and flowers
what pollen is in your soul        your agonies
how regimes plunged into your bones
                and became the ink in your pen
and sculpted your love stories your souls
a cup of dark chocolate its aroma wafting
        on Victoria street      the street I walked
a few steps with you        and imagined
your revolts and victories, imagining the poem lost
in translation rising like an inviolate city on your pristine page,

your poems          your poems breathing
in and out the universe       order no different from chaos
no different from your soul's panting
no different from your violet emotions or red intellect
no different from your prayers no different from your politics no
differentfromyourGodlessdeitynodifferentfrom

you write *to*                    me today,
you *write me.*          *A reader will read us one day.*
Yes. Your waiting is over.

Play on Magda Carneci's book title *Chaosmos.*
*Write* is the major trope in both poets' work.

# Lotus Feet

*for Zhang Shen*


Whatever the narrative whatever the century, she shrinks:
these are the feet of the sentence laid out bare;
a tale to tell, tall feet between the crushed bones of centuries; between
the tendons of Tang, Han and Song—language is pompous ballooning
for a conquering mind: *Five Dynasties and Ten Kingdoms* ended in a Song
so it seems, a mouthful of syllables jingling in the mouth, names of
dynasties: Liang Tang Jin Han Zhou Wu Wuyue Win Chu Shu;
long long lines of glory; phallic strides, mountainous thrusts
in Art; this is one unbroken uncrushed narrative.
But something is shrinking imperceptibly.
Beauty is in the eye of the
masculine beholder whose gaze says make her
small small smaller till she cannot
stand; so perfect so beautiful so dainty,
imagine moonbeams for feet
and lotuses for footprints. A
mere four inches—and
the male ego
erects
in desire.

*I am a teapot*
*I hiss, I pour a bitter tea*
*on my dainty feet!*

*On my dainty feet,*
*I hiss, I pour a bitter tea!*

# In the Yagna of My Dreams

*for Draupadi*

Strike! My heart calls,
exile me from this kingdom of hatred
to the odor of the unknown,
bred to start a war, instead
show me a destiny of love's
maze of marigolds,
a new melody sizzles in my bones,
separate from my father's anthem of revenge,
in this *sabha* people like pausing clouds before rain,
by my side, my father, revenge souring his breath, waiting
for the strike of the arrow to its mark—
first step to his mission—this irony of ironies! My Swayamvaram,
*Self-chosen! Ha!* My destiny was drafted a long time ago,
I stepped out of a fire fully sculpted by my father's slithering rage.

It is not the rainbow arch of the bow
or the marriage of your pupil with the pupil of the fish,
it is the rippling arrow of your arm, the tree-trunk of your back,
the tanned curve of your cheek that sends a shiver through me,
I curl like a vine tendril, wanting to fit in your curves, be claimed.
When you drew your arm back, all of time drew back and I vaulted to
the source of my being, and found a new reason to be,
when your muscled arm pointed upward,
it slashed me like a sword. You stepped forward.

You stepped forward. Time condensed:
your thigh's hazel sheen in the thin muslin,
my breath taut as a snake about to strike,
a possible world of intimacy parted my legs—inadvertently,
the smell of my jasmine garland exploded in my body.
You pulled the string.

You pulled the string, I vaulted to the sky for the last time,
How innocent I was! How was I to know love's archway
loomed in the architecture of revenge,
someone was pulling us all that day on the strings from a greater bow,
I walked into the future, my unbound tresses smeared with blood,
a black wind blowing in the land for eternity.

# Mirabai Calls to Manuela by the Silla de Paita

*for Manuela Sáenz*

Come sit with me by the Silla de Paita
by the Pacific's gossiping waves,
where the wind is a bow throwing arrows.
I call you now in this time of tyranny,
Dame-of-the-Sun, bold, bold woman,
shining medal on pan-America's breast,
I roll out a red carpet for you,
let us exchange notes of our lovers,
show each other our love-bites,
call for Krishna, Bolivar,
galloping on the horseback of our bones.

We embroidered our hearts with stars of love,
turned our backs on 'husband' and threw a garland
on the neck of a chosen one,
we exiled ourselves from the sanctuary of prescribed bliss,
for the chaos of an uncontracted passion,
walking barefoot on a road of thorns.

We bled.

Your story a sword in freedom's arsenal,
my songs on the wind,
step out of the mirror Manuela,
sister of my smoldering heart,
your heart a volcano among volcanoes,
of the Pichincha, you lit them, they lit you.

Let us show the world once again how to love man or god,
how to light courage boldly like a cigar,
hold it in the mouth in society's face,
teach us how to spin like a dervish lit by love,

Come soon Manuela for I am lonely,
I do not understand these times of gold and gravity,
History heralds my devotion for
the love of the dark-blue flute player
who stains eternity with his blue spirit,
But I confess, I asked for eternal enslavement to a God,
And you, you dared love a mortal man,
your heart a port-of-calling for love,
crazed with a desire for freedom,
you showed us love is not illegitimate or unethical,
I know sister, your love is harder,
to pledge loyalty to what is strong and then declining,
you loved what is impermanent and frail,
you never forgot Bolivar's dreams,
they shone in your eyes when they faded in his,
you loved with a lighthouse heart
that could free a nation.
And I loved for my soul alone.

# They Cannot Persist in the Sunlit Room

*for Sylvia Plath*

Suddenly
I know
I am not Sylvia

I persist in the dark foliage of life
And if not snow, blood on snow, I live.

My pages are not mausoleums or
ouija boards, walking tours among tombstones
where spirits moan, every poem a medallion of madness
        I live, inside another compass
not words of flint, steel, iron
        the soul's vomit.

Sentence-veins with poisoned blood
fissured stanzas, hack ed rhyme

poem-whorl, poem-nub

        hyphenated madness

Never, will I create a dark sky
glittering with cancerous constellations

This, I gladly confess
like syllables stressed as in:

I know I am not Sylvia.

Even though, I've dipped my nib
in the dark ink of her well
and know the magic of incantation
for the repetition of blue-throated names
        runs in my blue veins
and use the odd metaphor

I am not Sylvia when I use my pen.

I've been a woman sobbing on my bathroom floor
I've seen the soul's shine ebb and die
I've hoped on many days I could quietly fly
And my mind's buzzed with a swarm of bees
a chromosomatic mess
I've been a hanging woman from a noose of an ancient culture
daily demeaned
And the voices like a flock of vultures
(I'll tell you an open secret:
Women pluck other women's bones clean.)

       Still, I am not Sylvia.

I've walked to the edge of a river in my mind
many times
filled my pockets with
       stone-heavy poems
and the river returned my face as Medusa

And the dark water streamed upward:
     a *trisulam* to the sky,
    and I heard a black goddess command

       Live!

I am sane as rice on banana leaves
the alphabet engraved on skull

And even though my mind is not steady as
the hull of a ship
        and the world like a pack of thieves
 conspires to take my life
only a muslin sail in the wind
I will not behead myself,

A self, sieved painfully through
the mesh of this life

        I live.

# Memoranda for Baama

*for my paternal grandmother*


1.

Here was the hip, here the heart, here the heel,

how small she is, was, in the length of these mounds of ash,

in the contours of my remembrance, she is awash in gold-ochre dust,

she knew the language of dust, this grandmother of mine,

her wisdom was a settled pain.

Incense-roads,

slumberous moon,

shroud-sky,

screeching crows,

sauntering dogs,

glass-eyed Shiva:

lord of the cremation ground,

small-as-a-fly father,

woman in a Hindu crematorium,

I, anomaly.

Like Sita, so many said of her,

untouched, unburnt by samsara,

(like Sita, she had her sinews of steel, she survived,

her tongue was sharpened when it delivered honey.

She died peacefully too as noble souls die, they said.)

She had nobly walked, they said,

from the bedroom to die on a settee

in the hallway to spare my aunt

the cleansing rituals in the bedroom.

The priest scraped her bones and ash,

into a terracotta pot round as Ganesha's belly,

deftly tying a string around the red cloth flap,

from one womb to another she went.

2.

Walking to her backward in my umbilical memory:
ramshackle shed, rumbling machines,
the stench of cow dung,
coolies ambling around,
dark faces dusty with the ochre powder,
she had worked along with them at times,
in the dark ante room, slight unlit candle

in her new white widow sari,
*sans* bangles, *sans* botu, *sans* mangalasutra, *sans* everything,
they bled whatever color they could from her heart too,
I knew then I could feel hate for a country,
the way it was dark matter that could bend a woman's light.

3.

The stories adorned her lips like marigolds blooming on a tree,
we lay on mats in the summer heat,
her hair a voluminous white spiral or
a hanging loose plait like an albino snake,
there was a flavor of longing in her voice,
a woman's yearning for an embrace
masked in devotion,
stories from this movie or that myth …
I remember the leaking longing in her voice.

4.

My mother a raging demoness,
every cell suffocated with memory-gunk,
unforgiving, hating her marriage, her husband, her fate, India,
woman pounding woman like grain in a black *rollu*,
familiar epilogue: my grandmother always left,
with a bundle of clothes or her cheap suitcase
and unspilled tears in a sunflower auto,
and we children remained ashamed of our mother
and the rituals of family,
never did I know then my heart was being prepared as a torch
to carry the story onward,
I too would know this rage one day that can consume a woman's cells
and burn sky-high obliterating rain,
I would be Medusa, turn the living to stone.

5.

Gentle parchment in a frame,
outside, an antiseptic road full of metaphors,
the overstorey of oaks is a sanctuary,
I wonder, what is the language of the trees?
Whom do the berries summon with their redness?
Does the sky mourn our stories?
Her life was hard as granite,
her hands calloused with the scrub of the years,
I picked a faded mango-yellow sari in memory of her,
Love comes frayed, it is used and uses for its own ends, it seems to say.

# The Rug Weaver

*for Clara Sherman*

They called her the 'rug-weaver', and 'mother-weaver'—the one who wove
the courage of her people. Grandmother Clara of the Hashtł'ishnii spun her
clan's memories by the lantern of day and the black tresses of night. From
her fingers the wool flowed singing a lullaby. When she spun her rugs, the
diamonds rose like pyramids on the loom, boldly triumphant. She was crone
so she could play a jaunty song on the harmonica smiling like a young girl.
This woman knew how to make melodies from the wind's secrets and the
earth's rhythms. She knew the earth's language and, still, man's soul was free
as a song in the wind.

There are names for almost everything, we learn,
the wool gliding through her fingers as a river held by loving banks,
her fingers go over and over smoothing bumps
as our minds go over memories till we are free of their abrasion.
In deft motions she *cards* the cloud-like wool, coaxed to long tendrils,
vine of memory fluid in her sturdy fingers,
shell glasses, face furrowed like a ploughed land, the years have left ridges,
but her eyes hold still like a meditating Buddha,
and her smile is wide enough to encompass loss,
the breadth of plundered land,
she spins Ganado red diamonds pirouetting in the wind of time.

*"Go easy, your arm, your hand feels it, knows it ... right here, the wool cries."*
*Let us never stop loving the earth, river, wind and sky.*

And our story continues. As she wove, she spoke about another weaver, the mother weaver of us all. How she wove the canopy of the sky, the waterfall of light and the tunnel of night, then the golden glimmering stars, and the whirling planets, how her loom glittered with the cosmos. And how finally she wove the destinies of men all through time. And how she wove with fingers of love on a loom of eternity. When a rug was ready, she unstrung it and wove again from the beginning, going *tap tap tap*.

This poem's format took its cue from the article by Anthony K. Wenster, 'Who reads Navajo poetry and what are they reading? Exploring the semiotic functions of contemporary written Navajo.' In general, Navajos that I have worked with classify poetry as *hane'* ["story, narrative"] and not as *sin* ["song"] (Webster 2009). Although some poets – Luci Tapahonso, for example – often insert songs into their poetry. This practice, of inserting songs into a narrative, resonates with Navajo oral tradition (see Webster 2011b). https://www.tandfonline.com/doi/abs/10.1080/10350330.2012.693298?scroll=top&needAccess=true&journalCode=csos20

"Go easy, your arm, your hand feels it, knows it … right here, the wool cries." Quoted from Clara Sharman's YouTube video on carding and weaving.

# Moon-gazing Bird

*for Meena Kandasamy*

Rage has no caste, needs no algorithm,
light a pyre with it
of chopped thumbs and scripted dreams,
replace the world with poetry,
put your basket down

for
on new moon nights Meena
the moon's light is in your poems.

The poem references the following poems of Meena Kandasamy: 1. 'Ekailaivan', lines: *You don't need your right thumb, / To pull a trigger or hurl a bomb.* The poem is a dig at the Brahmin guru Drona who demanded the sacrifice of the right thumb of low-caste Ekalavaya, so that he would not surpass his favorite pupil in archery. 2. 'Moon-gazers', lines: *I become that moon-gazing bird on new moon nights,/I sing the saddest songs of all time, I never ask questions ...*, 3. 'Six hours of chastity.'

# This Is Where the Hair Fell

*for goddess Katyayini*


Scribble of an alley of outstretched beggar-bowls,
shivering triangles, saffron flags flutter,
turmeric stains sindoor smears squelch milk honey incense—
the messy religious memoranda in the sanctum sanctorum,
the gong heavy in the hand the lift the fall the reverberation
on the map of the palm, the shiver of this thread of awakening,
*Nandi* embodies our waiting for a God made of stone,
alive to his eye, alive to the circumambulations of faith.

*he, unloosened with grief in the cosmos, mourns,*
*his arms growing empty to the relentless work of the discus,*
      *her body-parts falling, temples rising on this desecration,*
        *the finality of release sends him*
*to an inner world beyond realms we don't know exist … till*
*she born again, mountain-girl, his name on her first breath*
*awakened him with her penance and devotion.*

We're hooked to this first grand love story born with the stars,
to these stories that erase Freud and science,
Here! In awe where the hair fell,
Here! In the timeless fracture of selves,
Up here, he waits, fiercely-mustached lingam
stoned in grief, and senseless with faith devotees prostrate,
cornucopia of marigold and melodies of rose petals,
something trembles within the hoops of cellular remembrance.
           To her we go: swallowed by the gullet staircase
              descending
    to the smoldering heart of our own being it seems,
    the fires in lamps are little whisked meteors,
    leaping away fiercely in the air,

her macabre presence, something horrifically real,
startled by her eyes that hold us as pinpoints of stars,
here hope can bloom like a blood-red hibiscus.
she nails it in the subterranean—*take back the dark feminine.*

# Rise

*for Turkish women immigrants at the Raindrop Center*

The air has the color of courage,
the table waits like a country to be taken,
the room is a manuscript of many longings.

The spices of new names and ingredients flounce
their skirts, toss their heads and make grand entrances:
Börek, Ay çöreği, Lahmacun, Sumak, Peynirli poğaça, Kalburabastı.
In the womb of round-bottomed glasses honey colored chai serenely asks:
*Where do we come from, how are we here, who are we?*
Quietly, the flour waits the modest mistress of them all, her
age unknown, old crone of eons, her cheeks are unblemished.

"I am going to make the most powerful food,"
Saltik says, smile warm as the inside of an oven,
She's in charge, and—her mother, grandmother
singing ancient chants and hushed lullabies
speaking the language of bread through her,
soon the women's fingers
like tapping heels, dancers in a row,
heads bobbing like Valentine bouquets
like pianists, they tap tap and fly,
like drummers, they pound,
they make the flour sing like mermaids to a shore,
they cajole, plead, pound, reap and meet,
tease and toss, the flour surrenders,
these fingers know, yes, they know,
wordless secrets flow,

in this room where people slip in and out
of the fingers of many countries,
the air watches as water with a silent tow,
the fingers glow,
with the secrets of what makes things rise,
what makes things live, what can quench
our thirsts, and hungers, the things women know
that pass down quietly through
the blood century upon century …
as if they know that Time too is like this—
flaky fillo sheets.

A life in the end is what happens between the layers,
what we fill it with, the appetite with which we bake it,
makes it rise.

# Ants

*for amma*

Home is a bird on a wire with the possibility of flight into dark woods or a patchwork of sky: It is the story of a daughter who had ants for pets as a child on one continent. On another, in Hyderabad, shallow breaths from resisting the inner matrix of mother; the serpentine struggle of the cellular to outdo itself, woeman

becoming woman, and the woman in woeman's eternal dance inching toward gravity-free leaps. Home is the first battle zone always wet with the mother's blood; umbilical trail present even in new woods. Under her feet continents bloomed as lotuses. Hyderabad, that teeming city, gave her dreams surreal as blue ants.

by day, hypnotized out of the jar of earth, vicious ants trailed like dripping tar. Meandering meridians of a woman's destiny — her mother's sweats and nerves in Hyderabad's sun, furious as a chariot in war. Her escape from home to an inner labyrinth of somber shady woods, lost in underground mazes to distance her mother's

frenzied toiling above. Mostly, it was her mother's home. Her father silent as an anthill, his words, dark ants, surfaced as guerillas nested in dark woods. How could the daughter now as a married woman not recall the relentless heat and ants in that house as only pests? Snow now white as gammaxene — a hybrid heap of memories haunts — the cumulus of cities: Hyderabad Melbourne, Baltimore, White Plains, Austin. Madder than the hatter she feels transiting from house to house. What did the mother make of this child gentle with ants? She clung to the image like a grain of sugar. Now woman, the daughter fought to fly in spite of plummets in the woods.

torn-winged, the futile
fierce flutters that would not falter — a second best life! Shrapnel sticks — Hyderabad. The first war is the war that never ends. Can women ever cease perceiving their 'tragedy' as 'Mother?' They must be crushed — trailing memories brittle as ants, she hopelessly hopes to erase the thread that leads home.

# Portrait of a Woman Poet

*for anonymous*

She was beautiful, fluid as night,
poems branched as tridents raised in battle,
circuitous as conches of hidden murmurs,
a childish voice enamored and narcissist,
her poems drifted as nails,
trails of silk and flags of womanhood,
the obsession with death; the romanticizing of madness and its
imitation; she was sane as a sunset falling into a habit of night,
Once they fished her from a lake; she came alive
like a phoenix; it's the others around her who die daily,
a hundred deaths a day to keep her alive.

# Sakhi

*for the courtesan friend, 'Untitled', a painting by Kartik Trivedi*

A cornucopia of green leaves,
"Delicate as a woman's chastity"
                    the old poets would say,
each sleepless leaf an eye rimmed
                              with red kohl.
Her hand adjusts a crimson flower
        like we adjust life when someone is gone.
Her eyes are slumberous, downcast,
        speaking of the stealth of love.
Her three bangles are red mouths
        asking for fulfillment.
Her lips are boats about to make a
                journey to a known land.

The friend is poised by her ear,
faithful confidante, we catch her life
                    sideways,
        crescent moon she is thirsting to be filled.

Against this suffusion, whispers alight,
                in the air like fireflies.
Think Shakuntala, think Radha,
Then, think the *Sakhi*,
        think love sublimated to friendship,
think of what unknown beats pound her heart.

# Requiode

*for my daughter Anannya*

Desire
whittled
to needle
point
intent—
this
delicate
embroidery
we
stitch,
*no other.*

I overwrote astrology. Where is he now?
Perhaps walking backward from the earth, my son, I never think of him.
Why did I want a Girl?      Why does the sky want a sun?
To will a dawn I suppose,        to break out of itself and shine
                                        and show her own shimmering wound.

For nine months I whispered *Girl,*      every breath a flower, at the end of
nine months
I walked in a garden of my own desire,
How could the Gods have not smelt this perfume—Girl.

The moment came; my body many torn petals my mind undone; many
fluttering wings of a moth
consumed by the flame of my body,      life lay warm at the edge of metal,
at the edge of knives the color of moonlight,      the blood.

A canvas of steel gray and helpless blood;       duotone monolith of birth in a
hospital room,
and I so alive,       so alive that I knew prophets crowded in that room,
                    and blessings dropped like satin or flowers or light,
my spirit soared to one point of gratitude for God,
for Life, for being woman …
Thank you …
not one ravaged curse.
How could this bloody boon given be anything but woman?

❦

In a neat poem of
three-layered elegance
like a hazelnut wafer

a metaphor turns up
like a man in a kilt on
a beach playing pipes

A child appears like that
in your three-layered life of
poetry, marriage, spirituality or

India, America, identity or
marriage, love, work or
loneliness, poetry, fatigue

Just like that one day
wearing a kilt
or some incongruous costume

all her own, armful of pipes
and lung power to wake the gods
and your own sleeping heart.

When you were not quite three months old,
      your hair straight as a drizzle,
With the deep knowing of a mother I said,
        "She will have curly hair."
Twelve months streamed by. Then we awoke to step into a wood of riotous
curls.

You stepped out of babyhood as well with a dark halo around your head,
   a fiery, fierce spirit, solid, sure, happy
   like a gypsy, strong willed, loving to dance,
   loving music, you play us like tambourines,
   we never knew so many wheels turned in our hearts

    and could make music.

I hold my daughter the way I did not know how to hold myself:
a petal, ant or snowflake.
I do not hold her the way India held me with her calloused and chapped
fingers,
I hold her with fingers of light.
As if the one chance for the earth to redeem itself is here,
   I hold her as a mother,
I let loose my revenge of Love upon the world.

I smell her hair hoping to smell
the moist monsoon, the Indian air,
instead I inhale the future,
hers is another matrix;
the ambiguous grid of a petal.

This I know of her: her body is pure as a bell,
Toes, the same size; an egalitarian kingdom,
Dark oil in her eyes, a sea sways behind
her conch ears; no ship of mine will sail on that sea.

My daughter: my footsteps gone ahead of me.

We danced madly one afternoon
in the disarray we had become used to.
The center island pushed against the wall,
uneven surface beneath our feet,
the workmen's voices in the garage
pushing padding into the walls,
this was the time I knew the house would go
and we too—where, not known but accepted.
I wore a trench coat over jeans and spotted clogs,
she wore a red turtleneck and pinafore,
And the CD charged the air with
*Raindrops keep falling on my head*, and *American Pie*.
In the scene was also a Winnie-the-Pooh umbrella.

There was no name to this dance of melting,
me into my daughter, she into me,
the anklets sound into the air, the house became
ageless, soft as a newborn's limbs wet with birth,
I danced through my lineage, the coils of DNA
and their heavy bearing, I danced beyond being Indian,
Brahmin, immigrant or outsider,
the raiment of identity, color of skin or lens,
And with us in that room was my mother dancing
with me in her memories, or as how she would have
liked to have danced with me on another continent shaped
like a crescent almond croissant,
And the house held us as the air holds kites.

Our home, a newborn calf,
often rearranges itself on its fours,
like pieces of glass in a kaleidoscope,
not in the same place, things displace,
poems in cookie jars, socks in envelopes,
mittens in letter-holders, she loves
to wear her clothes backwards.
Houses that have children are keys
opening locks they aren't supposed to open,
the hours turn up where they shouldn't,
a world of words written backwards.
Only the displaced seems resolute in purpose,
red stains of tulips in a ground of concrete,
child in the unease of marriage.

She insists on 'mummy,' or 'mommy,' or 'mom.'
I wince and claim 'amma'—this word—chord
of lineage—this word—river running into sea.

We spar daily in this hierarchy of sounds, language
our capers on the floor of two continents.
Rich with the sounds of her anklets, the air
shimmers with wind chimes to her every move.

'Go away,' 'I don't like you,' sounds sharp as a mouse-trap
closing on prey. I become a mountain, looming censor
of sounds to be said, not said, at three.

Also come the daily bevy of *I love yous*—a sound around
which bloom entire fields of tulips in which I dance.
I anchor my entire existence for the sound of her laughter,
she grasps a joke, it skips clumsily through a white topsy-turvy.

From this her mouth—small dark cave, mysterious orifice,
the provenance elsewhere—sounds slip through, inchoate clues
to the moist clay of herself, these are the days I believe truth
may have the color the cluster of dark purple grapes, the hours
are like piano keys, and poems don't ache with loneliness.

the house is her,
till she came we inhabited
geometric squares and rectangles
softened at the moment of her birth,
the walls began to unfurl as petals,
we gave off a new fragrance,
the doors opened as envelopes filled with money,
the stairs were stairways; all definitions expanded,
the house became the moon revolving around her,
she our earth, our sun, never mind she was born
in the dead of winter, she was fire, she was hearth,
she the prophet whose teachings I learnt through
my expanding heart; there is no dark side to this,
no irony, no appeasing the cynicism of this century.
To leave this house is to leave her history,
as time delivers us first from heaven,
then from the body of our mothers,
then from the body of our country,
then from the body of earth,
free.

## Your Story

*for Kamala Das*


You pulled weeds from underground
unpleated the years in poems, peeled yourself
as an onion wanting the naked center
your poems rode fierce chariots
clattering under a granite tradition
your womb like a *chakka pazham* teeming with
achenes of desires.　　　Harbinger　　trumpet　　pen.

You knew
women are fields filled with seeds
sowed with a mother's latent vengeance
a father's blind eye
a husband's need　　a woman's stories.

How then　　　　why then　　　　when then
the pilgrimage of disrobing　　　to　　　black-shrouded body
how did you slip through the crevices in your story?

# Bolokoli

*for Astur*


Welcome to the world little girl
cut cut cut cut cut cut cut cut cut cut
cut cut cut cut cut cut cut cut cut cut
cut cut cut cut cut cut cut cut cut cut
200 million times cut cut cut cut
cut cut cut cut cut cut cut cut cut cut
cut a clitorodectomy, infibulation, excision
200 million makes many constellations
constellations of 30 cuntries, cut-cuntries
nicked pricked pierced incised scraped cauterized.

de-petalled
capped
pruned plant
you're a sewn gunny bag little girl
you're clean and pure now little girl.

here's a lollipop!
hush little girl hush hush
don't talk little girl don't whimper
don't urinate, don't bleed
don't moan in pleasure
much much, much later.

keep your sunrises unseen
your tidal longings secret
be clean closed unseen.

What's that little girl?
louder little girl …

*fuck you fuck you fuck you*


*FGM in the Bambara language spoken in Mali means washing your hands, a purifying phrase.*
*Astur, Somalian girl's name meaning to cover or conceal*

114

# For a Certain Kind of Woman

*for the ones I can't be*

*A woman will be exalted in heaven by the mere fact that she has obediently served her husband.*

*They (women) pay no attention to beauty, they pay no heed to age; whether he is handsome or ugly, they make love to him with the single thought, 'He's a man!' ...*

*After her husband is dead, she may voluntarily emaciate her body by eating pure flower, roots, and fruits; but she must never mention even the name of another man ... By being unfaithful to her husband, a woman becomes disgraced in the world, takes birth in a jackal's womb, and is afflicted with evil diseases ... By following this conduct, a woman who controls her mind, speech and body obtains the highest fame in this world and the world of her husband in the next.*

*—Manusmriti, ancient legal text*

There's a certain kind of woman I fear,
wound in traditions and piety,
rouged with a meticulous attention
to refrain from bringing attention to herself,
tattoos of Brahmin caste and culture—
the botu, mangalsutra, bangles, toe rings,
a high-necked blouse veils her flesh,
her gait like a lolling elephant,
her braid a flag of her piety and virtue,
oiled, flattened, obedient, not a wanton wisp flutters,
she is demurely beautiful; her laughter is neither loud
nor raucous, she addresses her husband as *'andi'*,
affectionately bossy, she fussily puts up with his less adorable traits,
so saccharine is her tone the air becomes diabetic,
she is modest, an empress of her domestic domain,
her intellect is well reined utilized only for earning,
her studious simplicity is practiced to perfection,
her plain face of no make-up is exhibit A.

She is emboldened in her husband's bedroom like a Khajuraho statue,
in the morning she is virginal, her children are birthed,
a gift from the Gods, not from the lust in her body,
she knows every Sanskrit sloka and mantra,
she observes fasts and vrats,
she is respectful to elders, she wins their approval,
especially the grand patriarchs
are managed with such efficient sweetness,
they become blind to her failing—the burnt dal is overlooked,
she is a perfect PRO,
beloved to all, she is faultless,
her husband is a little snug ring on her finger,
so smug, he doesn't know he is being worn,
thinking he wears her,
this is a couple who have a passport to Hindu heaven.

She can make a 7-layer kaaja to perfection,
a pulihaara and pulsu, have the right amount of tamarind,
a doting mother she keeps her children in line with a look,
she is known to the temple priests and volunteers,
weaving delicate jasmine garlands on weekends,
the tulsi is sure to be in a pot by a window,
she keeps the flag of Sanatana dharma flying high,
she could be a badge for the BJP,
her girly voice puffs up a man's chest
and her recipe for womanhood tightens his loins in desire.

She is never bitter, she shuts out the 21st century,
she takes all of us 5½ centuries back,
she personally immolates other women who
are responsible for the air she breathes.

Instead of keys jangling at her hip
are many tiny sharp daggers,
she uses with precision to undermine other women,
she keeps a lot under lock,
her tongue is witty and sharp,
somehow, it is never noticed as bitchy,
she hoards goodwill and gifts from relatives
so precise are her feminine wiles and deliveries,
no one would suspect her
of anything but the finest sentiments and virtues,
it must be honey in her veins, not blood,
she is a golden lotus, she is a curse to other women.

She lives by divide and rule, she mastered Chanakya,
she does what she has to survive,
she will never support an abused woman in her family,
maintaining a smirking silence carrying the torch of patriarchy,
she is the kind of woman who makes a woman like me necessary,
she is the kind of woman who does not deserve a line of poetry,
so, this is poetry saying it in prose, as is.

Manusmriti, an ancient legal text is mostly known for the derogation of women.
   On December 25, 1927 at Mahad in Raigad district of Maharashtra, the burning of
   Manusmriti was moved by a brahmin named Gangadhar Neelkanth Sahasrabuddhe.

# Het Achterhuis (The Secret Annex)

*for Anne Frank*

Destiny is a hoop that a child rolls
oblivious on the pavement of her life,
always bigger than herself,
Unexposed yet to the labyrinth of human evil
my daughter is chatty, then quiet, then silent,
as we take the first tour this morning,
outside, a gray drizzle, the serpentine line of people,
too late in their coming and support.
The future is renowned to be a late visitor,
The names read: Edith, Anne, Margot, Otto,
Hermann, Auguste, Peter, Fritz,
numbers in the death lottery of the Reich.
Life is eternity at nine or twelve,
to live under a steeple of death,
to live huddled in whispers and soft footsteps,
this life is strange,
but as we turn the corners in the museum,
we turn in the spirals of time and see it has been so,
the pictures attest evil is the shadow of a friend.
Had he seen the years burgeoning in her
like flowers shooting from the mouth of a vase,
the fruit ripening, the bounce of curls,
the grave tones of her writing,
would he have halted the hard hammer of fate?
Had he known that in her young soul was a young Love,
Its tender stem pushing through the pure soil,
Would he have altered history?

We cannot know her final exit from life,
the books are silent, screams for her mother?
Was there relief?
Anne is neither the beginning nor the end,
we sacrifice our children in all our bungling,
any newspaper of any city is proof.
Go to Godhra! Go to Serbia!
Go to Afghanistan! Go Go Go!

# Recant at St Maximin

*for Eva*


So, this is the hinge-work of skin
in keeling flames, those the caves of eyes
slurping my pain,         pitchforks like
an alphabet staked        in the ground
     this is bone-sheen,
     like fishscale sear in yellow water;

        the eyes want more,
more pain, want        incantation to leave my lips to save myself
so I can be tossed back in again like a penny in a wishing well
of epileptic flames    but this is my mouth melting    smile-grimace
I mouth something like        forgiveness        curse
      these are words melting

    this is how orange feels.


      I pour myself out of myself molten lava,
      scarlet-ribboned skirt
city of lightning, an orange waterfall;
        body-liquid-pain one.


I burst into petals of the sun,
       I throw comets from my
navel, I am sprouting auburn blossoms
            I burn the day. I am hell,
   I am your air.
         Centuries, breathe if you can.

# One Snapshot

*for the women standing on Rosse Buurt*


Charming, cobbled Amsterdam street,
the canal a rope of gray glinting pearls,
in the smack of it, Oude Kerk,
the rumblings of organ music silent,
ponderous space of sin and good,
arches of wood and heavy floors of granite.

Outside, in a red laced window—
a statuesque apsara from Khajuraho in a neon bikini
ablaze on toned tanned thighs,

a panel of glass between her and me,
does she see me as I see her?
Does she want to see me as I want to see her?

She's in a dollhouse seated on a chair,
I'm in the hell outside,
each of us bartering what we can for comfort.

# Unsought Pickings

*for the African American slave women subjected to forced breeding*

The years between us are bolled Gossypium,
clawed realities spinning yarns—chilling truth *not* yarn,
Mandeville knew this was a beast-sprouting plant—
our *kutn*, your cotton—their currency of carnage,
I am told 'her' pain is not 'yours'
to articulate, share or voice; still, I seek her in
the blurred spirals of the feminine self,
my hand seeking her palm as a mirror,
perhaps, she imagined snowflakes to pick, snowflakes—
the white gold falling from the sky in the North,
instead, her fingers stabbed cotton like wasps,
the destiny of her people hewed her body
to a sickle seeking earth's arms more than sky,
did she think, "I'll be picking cotton till the sun is a hole,"
in the lament-soaked sky of waning blues?

Perhaps.

Did she seek answers in the liminal spaces of
unsought pickings blooming like soft cotton:
better the cotton-picking than
*de weddin' 'tween de cows and de bulls,*
than the decree from dank walls,
than the brooding air of muffled suffering,
than the damp wet cave of smothered pain,
than fingers and pubescence prying her open like a can,
than the unwilling rabbet of her private to his,
better numbing labor than the pinioning of air
pressing as a bale of hay,
the straw filling her mouth, throat, lungs,
her eyes sweeping the air like bats?

Outside, the sullen crushed sympathy,
like lifeless cotton with hardened seeds,
ears dialed to deafness for survival,
better her hands furrowed and perforated?
better her palms fissured with ancestral pain?

Did the moments of anger pile on stone by stone
to sift between unsought pickings
be a breeding woman than/
be fettered to a whipping post?
This better than a back striped like a field,
red petals of welts blooming to the sun,
a waste of dandelions around her drooping in shame,
staining her memory's notebook of incoherent rage,
a rage alive breathing like cotton?

Quote by a slave woman on crude eugenics practiced by slave owners from Thelma Jennings,
   'Us colored women had to go through a plenty: Sexual exploitation of African American
   slave women,' *Journal of Women's History*, Johns Hopkins University Press, Volume 1, Number
   3, Winter 1990, pp. 50; 45–74.
Guineamen: cargo ships for transporting slaves.

# She's Speaking

*for Kamala Harris*

*I didn't listen. And the people didn't listen, either. And we won.*

—Kamala Harris

The knee of a sewn conscience
compressed the country's gullet,
the country, a vulva cleaved—
in two, a salvo of wounds burgeoned
from the fruiting body of one heart,

the alphabet fell from her garland,

these streets—ledgers of lies,
an unbalanced history.

> You sprang from the house of triangles,
> rising with the sap of two bloods,
> a smile sure as the stalk of a lotus,
> spoke with a voice chorded
> with the sinews of voices before you,
> for the petalled voices to be.
>
> Wield the thunderbolt of Athena,
> guide our hand to pen new anthems,
> be the lungs for a forgotten dream,
> color the white house with Holi colors,
> help women sleep in their bed
> blanketed with stars, bathed
> in the nectar of skin,
> let hope again be a majestic elephant,
> fertilize our awakening on your petals,
> show us how from mud we can rise,
> teach us your chant *We did it, We did it,*
>
> > *We do.*

Kamala is the lotus in Sanskrit, the emblem of the Goddess Lakshmi.

124

# Glossary

| | |
|---|---|
| Annamayya kirtanas: | 15th century Telugu composer of devotional songs in praise of Lord Venkateswara, a form of the Hindu God Vishnu. |
| Avakai: | mango pickle made with spices, oil and red chili powder. |
| Brahmin Niyogi: | Telugu upper caste traditionally holding Vedic knowledge in positions of priesthood. |
| Botu: | red mark wore on the forehead by Hindu girls and women. |
| Caw Caw: | crows feature in Hindu after-death rituals. The soul in guise of a crow is believed to eat offerings during the death ceremony. |
| Chakka Pazham: | jackfruit (in Malyalam). |
| Darbar: | court or reception hall. |
| Dusasanna: | member of the Kaurava clan in the epic Mahabharta, he notoriously disrobed his sister-in-law in public. |
| Ghat: | bank of a river. |
| Hala: | the cosmic poison held in place in Lord Shiva's throat for the safety of the world. |
| Jyoti: | name of Delhi rape victim concealed by the media as per law. The word means 'light'. |
| Kali: | a form of Durga, a black goddess, she embodies time, the void and the fierce feminine spirit. |
| Kanjeevaram: | famous silk saris made in South India. |
| Katori: | small steel bowl. |
| Kurta: | shirt/long tunic. |
| Lingam: | oval shaped symbol of Shiva representing generative power and the universe. |
| Log, dry shards: | funeral pyre. |
| Mangalsutra: | 'auspicious thread', a necklace tied by the groom on the bride to mark nuptials; it is worn by a married woman henceforth. |
| Masterji: | term of respect to address a teacher or senior. |
| Mehandi: | henna. |
| Paan: | betel leaves prepared with condiments and areca nut. |

| | |
|---|---|
| Pallu: | the uppermost part of the sari that drapes over the shoulder. |
| Papadums: | thin, crispy snack made from spicy lentil dough. |
| Perugu: | yogurt (in Telugu). |
| Radha: | beloved of Lord Krishna; symbolizes the individual soul yearning for God. |
| Rahu and Ketu: | respectively the lunar nodes of the moon symbolized by the severed body and head of the demon Svarbhanu. It is believed bad times occur in a destiny during rahu and ketu dominant times or during Saturn's reign in the natal chart. |
| Sabha: | grand hall for public gatherings. |
| Sakhi: | used as friend in this poem. |
| Sambar: | stew-like dish with vegetables, lentils and spices. |
| Savitri: | mythological heroine renowned for her matchless devotion to her husband that brought him back from the abode of Yama, the lord of death. |
| Shakuntala: | the heroine in Kalidasa's *Abhijñānaśākuntala*. |
| Shiva: | male principle in Hindu mythology and religion, one of the main Gods of the Hindu trinity. |
| Sindoor: | vermillion powder mark of married women wore in the parting of the hair. |
| Sita: | heroine in the epic Ramayana, paragon of chaste womanhood. |
| Sudarshan chakra: | discus weapon of Lord Vishnu that killed at his bidding and returned to him. |
| Swayamvaram: | ancient practice in which a girl selects a groom of her choice among many suitors. Svayaṁ in Sanskrit means 'self' and vara means 'groom'. |
| War-Khasi: | a tribe in the North-eastern state of Meghalaya in India. |
| Yogini: | female practitioner of yoga, female spiritual teacher or mystic. |
| Trisulam: | trident; three-pronged spear used by goddesses Durga, Kali and Lord Shiva. |
| Upanayanam: | initiation into Brahminhood for boys with a sacred thread-wearing ceremony. |
| Zikr: | or dhikr is the Sufi practice of remembering God by reciting the names of Allah. |

# Publishing Credits

Some of the poems in this collection have been previously published in journals, literary magazines, anthologies and chapbooks, or are due for publication in these formats in 2021. The versions in this book may incorporate slight alterations from versions published elsewhere.

## Journals and Literary Magazines (online and print)

*Usawa Literary Review; Poetry at Sangam House; Beltway Poetry Quarterly; Virüs* (Istanbul); *The Red River Book of the Poetry of Dissent; Punnami* (Telugu); *Mana Telangana* (Telugu); *Saranga* (Telugu); *Dragonfly; The Big Scream; Asian Cha; Sahitya Akademi Journal IE; en(compass); Wordmasala; South Asian Ensemble; Pratik; SIPAY; Bangalore Review; Dragonfly; Erosthanatos; Peacock in a dream; The Statesman; Walt Whitman Journal; Prachya Review; lifeandlegends; South Asian Ensemble; MAPS.*

## Anthologies and Chapbooks

*The Kali Project; Contemporary English Poetry by Indians; Cuckoo in peril; Ordinary; Open Your Eyes, the anthology on climate change; Singing in Bad Times: A global anthology under lockdown; Hibiscus, poems that heal and empower; Ordinary.*

## Blogs:

Enough <https://tlablog.org/2019/10/03/enough-by-usha-akella-a-highlight-from-the-power-of-words-conference/> 2019.

Reemergence, Not Enough <http://ourpoetryarchive.blogspot.com/2020/07/usha-akella.html> 2020.

*If you would like to know more about*
*Spinifex Press, write to us for a free catalogue, visit our*
*website or email us for further information*
*on how to subscribe to our monthly newsletter.*

Spinifex Press
PO Box 105
Mission Beach QLD 4852
Australia

www.spinifexpress.com.au
women@spinifexpress.com.au